It's a familiar scene. The door shuts, with you on one side, and your kids on the other. Now what?

Now you're a divorced dad. And with this practical, sensible new guidebook to part-time fathering, you can build meaningful, loving and lasting relationships with your children, even after divorce.

The message of the authors is clear: You can make it work! You need your kids as much as they need you, and you owe it to yourself—as well as to them— to make the effort . . .

## *DIVORCED DADS*

A Practical Plan with
Seven Basic Guidelines
*by*
MORRIS A. SHEPARD
GERALD GOLDMAN

Morris A. Shepard and Gerald Goldman

# DIVORCED DADS

## Their Kids, Ex-Wives, and New Lives

BERKLEY BOOKS, NEW YORK

DIVORCED DADS
Their Kids, Ex-Wives, and New Lives

A Berkley Book / published by arrangement with
Chilton Book Company

PRINTING HISTORY
Chilton edition published 1979
Berkley edition / September 1980

ISBN: 0-425-04614-1

A BERKLEY BOOK ® TM 757,375
Berkley Books are published by Berkley Publishing Corporation,
200 Madison Avenue, New York, New York 10016.
PRINTED IN THE UNITED STATES OF AMERICA

# Acknowledgments

*There are a number of people who helped us. However, we owe a special thanks to Ruth Anne (it was her idea), Chuck Taylor (the first outsider to believe in the idea), and Peter Desmond (whose editing helped make the idea clearer). Also, Honora Hammesfahr and Gale Halpern typed the manuscript with their usual alacrity.*

**To the sea of humanity:**

**Aaron**
**Anton**
**Heather**
**Holly**
**Jennifer**
**Kathryn**

# Contents

# Prologue

We are two divorced, middle-aged, middle-class fathers. Each of us has three preteenage children. Each of us is working out a new life with his children and former wife.

The new life consists of sharing full responsibility for the children with their mother. That is, for us up to half of every month the children live with their father, who is totally responsible for them during that time. It isn't always easy. Each kid has two homes, and there are lots of logistical problems. But the children are doing well and we have grown as fathers. These results offset the difficulties.

We discovered early in the separation that our children still needed us—at dinner, at bedtime, and during the night. What follows is an account of the techniques, triumphs, and failures of two divorced fathers trying not to be phantom parents. Our story begins with the recognition that the pattern of "father as visitor" or "father as Sunday hero" is not constructive. It then describes our development of a child-sharing plan that allowed us to be a natural part of our children's lives. While we live in different areas and social settings, our experiences with sharing our children have been remarkably similar. We've pooled our ideas to write this handbook for fathers who share our basic goals but who have yet to make them work. We hope our ideas will help you stay involved with your children.

Morris A. Shepard—Winchester, Massachusetts
Gerald K. Goldman—Brownsville, Vermont

# DIVORCED DADS

# 1
## *The Breakup*

You slammed the door. Your kids were on the other side. You got in your car and drove down the side street, and you couldn't find the freeway. Like a home movie slightly out of focus, scenes from your recent life fluttered before you, fogging your sight and judgment. You couldn't make sense out of what just happened, and you couldn't find the right road. So you pulled over to an abandoned gas station, took a few deep breaths, then you started the car again.

As you drove away that day, one thing surprised you. After all those sleepless nights, after planning farewell speeches, after all those days of sitting at your desk pretending to be working, after all those soul-searching talks with your wife, you still weren't prepared for the way your kids looked when you slammed the door.

The first night you probably had somebody with you.

1

But the time came when you were alone, when the reality really hit you. Maybe leaving your children reminded you of the time you jumped from the garage roof with that old umbrella, trying to be Batman. You had planned that flight as carefully as any test pilot, examined the umbrella for tensile strength, and then leaped. When you landed your feet stung like hell, and you had a lot of second thoughts. After a few days without your kids, you realized you were in for another crash landing.

Being a divorced dad is a traumatic separation. You've had separation experiences before as you grew up. Maybe you went away to school, or took a job in a different place, or put in your military service. Your push for independence evolved slowly and was shared with others. You phoned your parents (usually collect). You went home on vacations or leaves. When you got out of the service or school, you may have stayed with your family for a while until the next phase of your life got underway. And you could turn for help to a student placement agency or the GI Bill. But divorce is unique; it is a lonely, cold-turkey separation.

A day at a time you start to build your new life as a divorced dad. The habit of family is hard to break, and the chances are that there's not much help around. You're part of the nuclear family age. But you're alone. There's no old maid aunt for a little warmth and home cooking. No parents down the street with an empty bedroom.

You find that it's hard to communicate with your parents—they're upset by the divorce and worried about their grandchildren. Your friends either ask a lot of questions or become remote. Your boss realizes that something is awry. Your paycheck won't stretch. Things that didn't bother you before do now.

In general your life is centered around problems. You wake up in a strange place and can't find your shaving gear. There are a lot of new skills to develop, such as making breakfast, finding the cleaners and laundry, and figuring out how to see your kids and what to say. And for a while all these things seem equally important.

The court decreed cash payments and scheduled times to see your children. Keeping your end of the legal bargain is tough at first. You depend on the bank to look the other way when you're late with the house payment or have an overdraft. While the visiting hours or days may have seemed reasonable when you negotiated them, you could not have foreseen the new tempo of your life. You realize that the previously established times no longer fit.

You and your former wife will work these things out eventually. You will establish your good citizenship with the court and one day realize that you have more free time to reshape your life. With no daily responsibilities to the kids, a part of you feels freer, more youthful. Living in a society which places heavy emphasis on youth, feeling younger makes you feel more "normal." But you're still a father with ties to your sons and daughters, and you think about their welfare. How can you do right by them?

The court decree defines only the outer boundaries of the relationship between you and your children. By setting visiting procedures, the court has given minimal recognition to the fact that kids need to see their fathers. However, it knows nothing about what your individual sons and daughters need. You're the only one who can determine that, just as you are the only one who can determine how you will help them adjust and grow. What kind of a divorced dad are you going to be? You are at a fork in the road.

We both arrived at that fork and decided to stay heavily involved in our children's lives. That decision has greatly influenced the way each of us lives. We are now several years away from the slammed door, and we've learned a few things about handling the jolt. We didn't learn these things from the experts. Rather, what we know came from a lot of errors and few a successes. We want to emphasize that mistakes and triumphs both need careful scrutiny if a divorced dad is to be successful. Don't let anyone shrug off your concerns or imply that staying close to your kids is easy after divorce. It isn't. This will become clear as we reveal what we went through and then examine the ways we have kept our "divorced dad" lives in order.

# 2
## *Fast Food Fathers*

### SUNDAY HEROES

You can pick him out any Sunday. He sits opposite his kids in a hard, antiseptic restaurant booth. The children talk too fast and too loud—or not at all. Dad and kids resemble labor negotiators who want to settle the strike but believe their constituents don't. So there they sit, each hoping the other will find the solution. To be sure, both sides are uncomfortable in their cold, plastic seats, but neither is eager to end the familiar ceremony of hamburger, shake and fries. The "Disneyland Dad" has again begun his Sunday ritual at the temple of fast food.

Next you can find him at the puppet show, Marine World, or the local equivalent of Disneyland. He is mainly with his children at special times, doing unreal things. He supplies a lot of material goods and emotional cotton candy. To avoid confronting the realities of separation and divorce, he has planned a day full of carnival-like events. At the end of such a day, dad and kids might return to the same restaurant booth. Then dad makes one last valiant, usually unsatisfactory, effort to communicate.

This brief description of the Disneyland Dad is not meant to condemn fathers who find themselves with their kids at a restaurant booth on "visiting Sunday." Nor is the phrase an attack on the Disney enterprises; it emerged as a result of a particular conversation with one of the Shepard daughters. While being driven along the freeway in the San Francisco Bay area a few years ago, Heather Shepard (then age seven) decided to test the waters to see how far she could push the new separated-parent system. She tried to get her father to do something he previously would not.

Before the divorce, going to Disneyland was taboo in the Shepard family. If that sounds somewhat harsh, think about your own family for a moment and you'll understand. Most parents have at least a few taboos. Some families, for example, don't allow their children to chew gum containing sugar. Others pride themselves on governing TV watching. The Shepard kids' father would not let them visit Disneyland. To him it symbolized an extremely superficial form of family activity. He felt righteous; the kids felt deprived.

On that day in the Bay area Heather decided to smash the icon, or at least to chip away at it. Nearing the exit leading home to mother, she decided to go for the whole prize and queried, "Well, this has been a pretty fun day, but when are we going to Disneyland?" Thousands of freeway miles, I still remember clearly my answer on that Sunday night: "I'm not taking you to Disneyland— not this week, not ever. I wouldn't do it before, and I'm not going to do it now, dammit! I'm not going to be a father who only takes you to fairs and carnivals; I won't be a Disneyland Dad."

The apple had hit Newton's head; I had a "eureka" experience. Suddenly there were two words which stood for something I did not want to be. There was now a phrase which the kids and I both understood, one which evoked negative images. Thinking about what it meant to be a Disneyland Dad didn't make me feel good, but at least I had identified what was bugging me.

Having declared that being together only at "events" was not what I wanted, I realized there was a void. If we didn't do those things, what in hell would we do? What would or could be done with three small children, not much money, and no room at the inn?

While "Disneyland Dads" came from a conversation within the Shepard family, both of us found it a useful phrase. When we began to compare notes about being divorced and about the young children each of us was "sharing," the Disneyland Dad idea was a shorthand way to describe many of our mistakes. Later we applied it to other dads we saw in fast food emporiums in Boston and Vermont, dads who spent Sundays squirming in their seats trying to "get it on" with their kids. It became a device for measuring parental effectiveness and is widely used in the divorced-father subculture.

We use the phrase as an early warning signal. It is a way to check our dad/kid relationship, to make sure that we are not falling into new destructive patterns. Much like having your blood pressure taken, you should, if you are a divorced father, periodically check your Disneyland Dad quotient. Are you behaving like a Sunday hero? Do you see your children mainly at events or when they are ill? If so, your Disneyland Dad quotient is too high. You'll have to change if you want to improve your relationship with your kids and maintain your own emotional equilibrium.

Most divorced dads go through a stage of interacting with their children under unreal or awkward circumstances. If that's where you are now, if you're mainly doing carnival-like things with your kids and you haven't been able to define the kind of relationship you have with your children, chances are you're being a Disneyland Dad. We have seen it hundreds of times and we've done it, too. It is a rare divorced father who avoids it. This syndrome is usually the first stage in the divorced dad/kid relationship. It need not be a permanent condition, but some fathers never manage to move beyond it. If they don't, it is likely that they will cease being fathers. Their visits will become shorter and finally disappear.

## FOOTLOOSE AND FANCY FREE?

How does it all start? At first, a newly divorced father thinks of all those places his dad never took him. Because he seldom, if ever, got to go to carnival-like places, he figures they must be fun. Or he remembers all the exciting things he did with his dad. He probably forgets they were done over a whole childhood and weren't telescoped into one day. But because the divorced dad doesn't live with his children anymore, yet wants desperately to make them happy, he makes great plans for their time together. "We'll go to the zoo, visit the ships in the bay, go to a movie and then we'll have a treat." There is only a short time to spend with the children, so as much giving as possible is packed into the time: love, "culture," and excitement. Maybe these were things the Disneyland Dad didn't get enough of when he was a boy. Or maybe he planned to do many of these things before the divorce, but didn't.

Initially, Disneyland Dad does not create this awkward situation by himself. He, society, the courts, and his former wife have set up the process which almost ensures that the dad will drift into a stilted relationship with the kids. The divorced parents agree upon the legal settlement, which usually includes specific visiting days, hours, and rights. By carrying out the terms of the decree, the dad is forced to communicate with his children in a contrived way. He depends on dramatic activities, crowded stores, and restaurants, to provide the environment for their limited time together.

It's hard to break the pattern. Your own inability to understand what your kids want when they are with you in this new arrangement adds confusion and frustration. Your may be slow to realize that contrived "fun" is not helping your children or you. In fact, you may never get out of the pattern unless you understand how you got into it.

It probably started the first day you went to visit your kids after moving out of the house. You phoned and discussed the time and the logistics with your former wife. (During separation, there may be no formal visiting rights, but you want to see your children, are trying to reach out and to maintain some contact with them.) You miss them more than when you were away on a business trip. There's a new void in your life. Even when your marriage was ending, daily contact with your kids seemed good for both you and them. You feel gloomy and you try to think of "fun" things to do with them.

You probably have not had time to consider what you will do with your kids now that your relationship is altered. For the first visit you get the romantic notion of going to a circus. Then you find that the circus is not in town, so you settle for the next best thing, a place where there are clowns and food. Kids always enjoy McDonalds.

You know that you want to prolong the good time. You want them to associate your visits together with happiness. Hasn't everyone involved experienced enough unhappiness during the past few weeks? So after the hamburger, you go to the park. This fast-paced day works well because your kids are very excited about seeing you. Despite the care you took to explain the separation, they no doubt seriously considered the possibility they would never see you again. They have not had many frills in their lives lately, but now you are more attentive than before. When you combine your highly anticipated arrival with some exciting events and junk food, you surely have a winner. However, when you do it every weekend it becomes as stale as fast food three minutes out of the ultraviolet warmer.

When the separation takes place you move to a new apartment. Once there you quickly realize you no longer have adequate space for you and your kids. Even if you have enough space, it is probably pretty barren. You have few furnishings other than a bed, TV and coffee pot. You don't have a lot of cash to furnish the apartment now that you're making support payments and have just put down a deposit plus the first month's rent. The thought of entertaining your kids in an empty apartment in an unfamiliar part of town is depressing. Since *you* may not want to be there, you naturally turn to activities outside of the apartment when your children are with you.

During the early months of the separation you have doubts about breaking up the family. You're torn in many directions. You want some time to think about the impending divorce. You want to see your children. You want to be alone. Competing emotions surface during those first visits with your kids.

There may also be another woman in the picture. You said you'd see her on Sunday, or maybe she spent the night. Again you hesitate to bring your kids to your new apartment because you haven't yet resolved your straight image and your new liberated life. No room, little cash, another woman, and the need for time to think, all act upon you as you remember the promise you made to yourself when you moved out—my kids need me; I will see them as much as I can.

You became a Disneyland Dad because you were overwhelmed by the competing forces of a new life, one in which the old rhythms and patterns have been derailed. You want to be a constructive influence in their lives. Even though you don't live with your kids, you want to continue to be their male parent. But it's hard to develop communication with them when so many things are happening all at once. As a Disneyland Dad you only go through the motions of being a father to your children.

The kids can tell you're distracted. They soon discover that the milkshakes and movies are substitutes for conversation and involvement and being a real dad. But you can't depend on them to get you out of this. They're new at it too, and besides, they're only kids. They probably can't really express what is bothering them. Your first clue that the arrangement is beginning to lose its luster is when a child shows a lack of enthusiasm about being with you. He announces that he has been invited to a birthday party the next Sunday, so he won't be able to see you.

At first you feel betrayed. You tried to do fun things. You were consistent about visiting. But now, once again, you've failed. Even after trying so hard, you feel you've struck out with the bases loaded and lost the crucial game.

It isn't the whole game, though; think of it as the first inning. You can be more successful the next time at bat if you analyze what has happened in the harried days immediately following separation and divorce. Keep two things in mind: you're not the first father who's done this, and you can (and should) leave your Disneyland Dad days behind.

We have solid personal evidence why you shouldn't

go on being a Disneyland Dad, and at least one major study (discussed in Chapter 9) shows that divorced dads who have a more total involvement with their kids are happier than those who do not. That, simply, is our message: you and your children will both do better if you avoid being a Disneyland Dad. Here's how you start inventing a new divorced dad role.

## INVENTING A NEW ROLE

You isolate a few hours to be with your kids. You feel good about acting on your commitment to remain a viable part of their lives. But when you pick them up you realize the few hours you have together are only a warmup. (It's similar to the physical "loosening up" that takes place before any event. The pitcher heats up his arm on the sidelines while the infield throws the ball around; the guests at a party begin to get more lively after a few drinks.) When you lived with your kids you didn't need any time to warm up, to step again into their lives. You were already there when they woke and when they went to sleep. But everything has changed. It isn't a natural flow anymore. It's a series of steps, and sometimes you have barely reached the first step when it is time to take them back to their mother.

The frustration of never moving beyond the warmup phase was overwhelming when we first "visited" our kids. We used to drive to their homes and take them out to lunch or for a milkshake, trying frantically and with fixed smiles to cram all the loss of communication into a very short time span. It never worked. After about three hours we would return them to their mothers, give them one last desperate hug and say, "Don't forget that I love you very much." It was a feeble attempt at being a father.

12

After some months of unsatisfactory visits like these, we promised ourselves that we would never "program" another three-hour session. The search for the answer to the question, "How can I improve the *quality* of time spent with my kids?" resulted in a new arrangement. Now we always get beyond the warmup phase.

The first step in breaking the Disneyland Dad pattern is to separate thoughts of your children from thoughts about the divorce. Think about what you and the kids did before the divorce. Think about the times when you made them happy and you had a good feeling about it. What happened at those times? What were the surroundings? Were other people around? Chances are that your kids responded best when you did something uncomplicated. Maybe it was an early morning breakfast when the world was quiet, and you easily answered all the world's chicken-and-egg questions. Think about how your kids responded then and you'll understand what you should do when you see them next. Try not to think about court, lawyers, unpaid bills, and other women. Focus on your kids, not on episodic events or artificial places. Focus on what makes you feel warm as a parent.

You'll need to make a few changes to be successful, and the first change should be in the schedule. Sunday is not always the best day to see your kids. Change to another day, or combine an evening during the week with a weekend day. The reason is that your kids must be involved in your life during normal times.

Pick them up after work. Let them talk to you while you're fumbling through dinner or allow them to help prepare the meal. Take them with you when you go to the dry cleaners or when you talk with a friend about the next tennis match. Take them with you when you play tennis so they can watch. At the day's end, hold them while you watch the news on television and then make getting ready for bed a fun ritual.

Let your children in on your everyday life, however dull you think it may be, and make them a regular part of it. Youngsters like ritual; they feel comfortable knowing what is going to happen next. If they can set the table or make the soup, let them do it. While they're being helpful, they are also interacting with you and gaining new skills and insights. Use these seemingly empty times to ask questions about their day and encourage them to do the same about your life and day. Don't be quick to conclude that it won't work. Don't get fractious if they spill the soup or ask the same absurd questions several times. This is a new way of life for both of you and will take some time to work out.

Changing the schedule and involving your kids in mundane tasks will help them develop a sense of your life and their place in it. Some of these are symbolic changes, but there should be tangible ones as well. For example, your kids should keep clothes and toys at your place. An old chest or box to keep a few toys, paper, pencils, or other things they use to amuse themselves is a basic minimum.

Like adults, children need time to themselves to reflect on the events of their day. They should also have time to amuse themselves in your presence. Like you, they will get tired of the checklists of questions ("How's school? Which friends do you play with?") and will need quiet times to draw or to play with toys. Kids seem to do this best when they have some of the trappings of their daily lives around them. This may seem like a tall order, but as your child-sharing plan matures you'll eventually create a second home.

## RESTRUCTURING RELATIONSHIPS

Creating this new environment needn't be done all at once; in fact, it's best done gradually. You can't do it all by yourself, either. Making it happen is a process which should be shared. Watch for what your kids like to do best and then build on those things.

You must reach a balance between being a pal and a dad. Both of you must be clear about this. Leftover guilt from the divorce ("I'm a lousy father, I walked out on my kids who need me.") can cause you to act more leniently than you should. There are enough books about parents setting limits and kids needing limits to keep us from expanding on this subject. But whatever you philosophy of childrearing was before the divorce, try to operate in the same way now. Consistency is vital.

There are two ways you know that you have gone beyond the initial Disneyland Dad stage. The first is when you and your kids do something mundane together regularly. They fix the soup; you make the grilled cheese. Exactly what you do is not important. What is important is that you are doing something together that is done by most families. The second is when you have formally restructured your child-sharing arrangement with your former wife.

Being a Disneyland Dad has an impact on your former wife, too. She is aware of the kids' excitement when you are scheduled to arrive, and of their emotional low when you've left. Your kids' highs and lows will make them difficult to control in your absence. Your former wife senses that you are the bearer of good times while she represents everyday life. Also, during the Disneyland Dad stage, she probably punishes the children more than you, which is not an equitable arrangement. By shifting away from your role of "candy man," you will ease the pressure on your former wife and improve your relationship with her. By lightening the load of her childrearing responsibilities and not adding complicating highs and lows, everyone will benefit—your former wife, your kids, and yourself.

We believe that you, as a divorced dad, need more

than one day per week to become acquainted with your kids' lives. And they need time to do the same with you. You both must become less of a mystery to each other, and more regular time together is the way to do it. Your kids need an adult male to talk to about important (and seemingly unimportant) events in their lives. If all they get is a Sunday hero, they will have trouble relating to male figures as they grow up.

So you should try to gradually expand your one day with your kids to several days each week, with the goal being to spend approximately half their lives as children with you. Naturally, for a host of reasons, not all divorced dads can reach that goal. But remember, the goal is an ideal.

Achieving this goal, breaking the Disneyland Dad pattern, *does* involve swimming upstream. If you have any lingering doubts about breaking the pattern, do some additional carnival-like things and the doubts will soon evaporate. But don't interpret all that we have said as being anti-fun. We're all for fun, but not canned fun.

Totally breaking the Disneyland Dad pattern involves changing habits and socially prescribed behavior. It means becoming truly involved with your child for as much time as you can provide. It means ignoring the cultural sterotype of the divorced dad. Changing your behavior and challenging the accepted model is difficult. It won't happen overnight. Initially you may be uncomfortable with this approach, but you must keep in mind that you are responsible for other people. No matter what the courts have decreed, you are the only one who can take charge of the father/child relationship. It is a challenge.

You can't provide your kids with fantasies of what your life is like when you're not with them, or fill them full of fast food, and expect that you will have a real-life relationship. If you hope your kids will handle the

16

pressures of their later lives with strength and good judgment, you'll have to involve them in your life as a divorced dad at the earliest possible moment.

# 3
## *Divorce Training, American Style*

During the first stages of divorce you're expected to act like a Disneyland Dad. After all, as a married father you acted in a socially acceptable way. The chances are, for example, that when you were married your major role was to bring home the bacon. You weren't expected to cook it, serve it, or dispose of the grease. Now you're on your own and you relate to your kids in the same way that you did before, not as a homemaker, but as a provider and special events man. Only now there's no home or homemaker to go along with the special events.

Your training as a father, then consisted of mainly providing funds. Unless your former wife was a liberated woman, you probably did not cook, sew, or clean house. Nor did you participate very much in the actual rearing of your children. How many diapers did you change?

When you found a diaper soaking in the toilet, did you scream for your wife or did you take it out, rinse it and put it in the hamper? When you arrived home each evening, did you help with preparing the meal? In all likelihood you did none of these things. Maybe you would have if your wife had pushed. But she probably didn't, so during marriage your childrearing, housekeeping and other related skills atrophied.

After the separation and divorce, you need these skills. You need them for yourself and for your relationship with your kids. But it is a big leap from being only the provider to being the provider/homemaker. And society doesn't offer much help in taking that leap. For instance, how do the media portray divorced fathers? *The Odd Couple* comes immediately to mind. There are very few novels, stories, or movies which report what divorced dads should be other than cigar-chewing, house-littering, visiting heroes.

The problem is more than lack of skills and guidance, though. The divorced dad who wants to take an active part in raising his kids has at least two hurdles in the way—conventional wisdom and the legal system.

## CONVENTIONAL WISDOM

"Attila the Hun was from a broken home." This phrase from a recent magazine summarizes how society feels about the fate of a child of a divorce. It's axiomatic: children from broken homes are doomed.

Kids do suffer in a divorce, and many act out their parents' problems. But most people, including kids, suffer as a natural result of living. If it's not divorce, it's something else: battling parents, blemishes, or chronic asthma. Philosophers tell us that to be alive is to encounter problems, to suffer, and to survive. So it goes with kids who have divorced parents. They'll suffer, but they can overcome.

No one should interpret this view as, "Because everyone has to suffer, children might as well suffer from divorce, if that's what pleases the parents." We don't argue for divorce even when no children are involved. But if divorce occurs—as it increasingly does—then there are things both parents can do to minimize the suffering.

Take a brief look at what's happening to families, divorced parents and to kids. Few in our society will argue against the ideal of raising children in a two-parent home, one in which the parents are loving to each other and to the children. But with all the pressures our society places on the family, parents seem less able to maintain this ideal throughout their childrearing years. The statistics on divorce rates are familiar to all. By the mid-seventies, divorce affected one million American children under age eighteen. Over the last twenty-five years the number of split families has tripled. About half of the couples marrying this year will eventually divorce. Whereas formerly families stayed together for the children's sake, now they frequently part for the same reason. And that means a lot of children will be affected.

In most cases the mother gets custody. The courts follow the lead of the experts in child development. In order to minimize the child's confusion, these experts stress a one-home, one-primary-parent arrangement. That parent is usually the mother.

This conventional wisdom seems inconsistent. If most experts agree that children do best before the divorce when both parents are active in their lives, then why should the children be deprived of one parent after the divorce? Divorce does not ordinarily mean that the parents have stopped loving or cannot live with the children. It means the parents have stopped loving or cannot live with each other. Granted, the divorce will affect the kids.

But wouldn't the children's interests be better served if they had easy access to both parents?

Not so, say many experts. Sons and daughters going through the breakup of a family need all the signs of security they can get. With one foot in each parent's home, a child will supposedly feel insecure and confused.

Some psychologists believe that when kids divide their time equally between both parents they never give up hope that the family will be reunited. They may even come to see themselves as the diplomats between two bellicose nations. They may feel they have the power or the responsibility to make peace. Placing them (the theory goes) in this situation keeps them from burying the past and may inhibit their emotional growth. Sharing of the kids may have a similar effect on the divorced parents, the theory elaborates. Increased contact with the children and with each other may keep one or both parents from accepting the finality of the divorce, and by not accepting the divorce a parent may be depriving himself or herself of a new life. On an even darker note some child development experts hold that equal child sharing may be fraught with psychic danger, for when the parents are unable to resolve their emotional conflicts, they may try to use the children as foot-soldiers.

In most cases a kid loses a dad in divorce. This is so because, despite the growing exceptions, conventional wisdom tends to eliminate a clear role for the divorced dad and to make him (often unwillingly) a shadowy figure in his child's life. And the conventional wisdom has become enshrined in law.

## THE LEGAL HURDLE

At the turn of the century many state laws reflected the belief that the father was entitled to custody of his legitimate children. But now the opposite is generally true. What accounted for that change? We aren't sure, but it seems to be related to literature in the early twentieth century which emphasized the importance of the mother during a child's early months. This view, known as the "tender years doctrine," held that all things being equal, the mother was the more appropriate parent to retain custody.

During the first quarter of this century the courts began giving mothers custody most of the time. Some states tried to demonstrate that they would not punish the father under the tender years doctrine. New York, for instance, revised the divorce statutes to indicate that there was no *prima facie* right to custody. However, mothers continued to get custody.

Mothers now get custody about 90% of the time, probably because most judges are looking back to the tender years doctrine as a guide. They know of little or no research which might lead them away from that doctrine, so they do what they have done in the past.

The only exception to this pattern is the recent trend toward joint custody. Though slight, the increase in joint custody is a positive legal and social movement. Apparently some judges are aware that it often takes two parents, even in divorce, to rear children and also that dads, when given an opportunity, will participate in their kids' lives on a regular basis. However, before we jump with joy about this increase, it should be noted that joint custody is not easy to obtain.

The tender years doctrine is still very much in the minds and hearts of most of those associated with the courts. Some attorneys will not even take a divorce case in which joint custody is an issue. Next, both mothers and fathers are often threatened by joint custody or the rules under which it is granted. In one state we know of, for example, when joint custody has been granted and one of the parents wants to leave the state, he or she must petition the court and get the other parent's permission. Just the thought of such a rule and not the reason behind it can dissuade separated parents from attempting to get joint custody.

## JOINT CUSTODY

We believe the most important part of the argument for having either joint custody or an extensive child-sharing plan is that it *will help* the children resolve the divorce. Being involved with both parents will help kids face reality: their parents live in different places. They know that because they have experienced both places. Being involved in both parents' lives will help kids cope with the divorce. They will see both their mother and their father working out their new lives, doing different things with new people. Gradually the finality of the divorce will become clear.

In any case, it is very difficult for divorced parents— either under joint custody or an informal but binding sharing arrangement—to completely sever ties. Whatever the nature of their contact after the divorce, the parents have agreed not to depend on or to take care of each other. But that agreement does not extend to their mutual care of the youngsters. They are bound to each other as parents, whether they talk to each other once a day or once a year. To say that communication between two divorced parents about the welfare of their children will keep them from resolving their divorce is to believe that after the divorce the two former partners must never confront each other.

Granted, one or both parents can use the contact through their children to prevent the separation from being resolved. Child sharing then becomes an excuse for adult interpersonal problems; it is not being done to benefit the kids. However, we believe that sharing the children, if done with their emotional security uppermost in mind, can be a successful way of raising them. It's not too much to expect that two parents will muster the soundest parts of themselves for their children so that their kids don't get short-changed.

We believe that many divorced dads would like to and could be a more positive force in the lives of their sons and daughters if they had alternatives. They can do this by first building upon the previous relationship and forgetting the conventional wisdom, cultural stereotypes, and even the courts.

We do not view joint custody as a panacea for insuring that a divorced dad will stay involved with his kids. However, he should have this option. He should not be relegated to second-class citizenship. Most of the courts in most of our states do not now facilitate joint custody or child sharing. They should, however, be working toward allowing more flexibility when children are involved in a divorce. At the same time more experts, legal and psychological, should develop better data about joint custody and the sharing of children.

We believe that the health and stability of our kids is in no small part related to our continued involvement with them. We also believe we have, as a result of our child-sharing arrangements, become better parents. We'd like you to know how it was that we decided to stay involved with them.

## THE GOLDMAN STORY

"Whenever I walk through Scollay Square I look in the faces of the bums and winos to see if one of them is my father. I know he won't be anywhere else but a place like that 'cause, after leaving my mother and me like he did, he's got to be no fuckin' good."

Don, a troubled adolescent whom I saw regularly as a social worker in Boston, said that. Don never knew his father. He spent a lot of energy thinking about and searching for his dad. His inability to deal with his feelings about a man he might never even recognize led to enough antisocial behavior to put him in the courts and social agencies. Don was bright, engaging, and attractive. However, not knowing his father was the difference between the usual adolescent turbulence and behavior which resulted, finally, in incarceration.

At the time I knew Don, I was single. My parents were never divorced. My father died suddenly when I was seventeen, but I reached the late teens having shared a lot of time with him. While Don's feelings made a profound impression on me, they were hard for me to grasp totally. What would I be like if I never knew my dad? Well, I might be more cautious like my mom. I wouldn't have a temper which, when I finally let it out, makes me feel I could take on the whole world. If I had not known my dad, I probably wouldn't like waking at 5 A.M. to get a big jump on the day and enjoy seeing the sun come up. Nor would I take as much pleasure in playing outside or working with my hands. Don's expressions of frustration left me feeling helpless and sorry. Even if I turned into Bruno Bettelheim himself, I couldn't come close to filling that likeable, unfortunate kid's need.

The years went by. I married. We had a boy, Anton. We got divorced. On the day I moved out, I thought of Don and what he had said. I vowed that Anton would know me, warts and all. More years went by. I remarried. We had two girls, Kathryn and Jennifer. We got divorced. The reader may already suspect what it took me fifteen years to understand: I'm not much of a husband. But I'm not a bad father.

There are two reasons I'm not a bad father. The first is that my father centered a lot of attention on me. My dad and I did a lot of things together that were pleasurable. Moreover, my dad was a bit of a kid himself. Although he worked long hours, he was always playful and never remote. I knew he loved me and I knew that I entertained him. I still remember how it was between my dad and me, and that gets transferred to my kids. Whatever hard feelings both divorces engendered, I was determined to prevent their spilling over on the kids. Because of my own relationship with my father there was no question about removing myself from my kids. What I had learned as I grew up was that fathers and kids enjoyed one another. Fathers protected and provided for their children. I didn't learn much about being a husband from my dad, but he sure taught me how to be a father.

The second reason I'm not a bad father has to do with what I learned from Don. Don showed me what could happen to kids with phantom fathers. I never want that to happen to my children.

## THE SHEPARD STORY

Growing up in a small Ohio town, I knew very few kids whose dads were not with them, and no one who was divorced. Most people couldn't afford it. During my childhood there was no guide to how a divorced father might behave toward his kids. In the intervening decades and as my life moved from Ohio to Massachusetts, I met armies of divorced fathers who, for a variety of reasons, chose not to stay around their children. A highly mobile society made it possible for most of them to drop in on their kids from time to time, but that same mobility keeps many dads from being personally involved with their kids.

Conversations on planes, in motels, airport lounges, and after-work drinks with divorced dads gave me some grim images of men who were concerned about their children but who somehow let fatherhood take a back seat to their careers or to their social lives. Most kept the lid on their emotions.

When I first became a divorced dad, I thought a lot about my kids. How did I make the best of an imperfect situation for them? There was no help in my childhood experiences and mainly negative models from my peers. I went through libraries and bookstores coast to coast. I called a few family agencies but could not connect with anything that made sense. As a trained social scientist, I went looking for data to gather, interpret and analyze so that I could reach an informed conclusion about my kids' welfare. I even read some nationwide studies about child development. None of this helped. Finding and filtering data did not solve my problem.

My next reaction was to spend a number of weeks avoiding my kids, working 70 to 100 hours a week, making the rounds of the singles circuit or dinner parties. I also played a lot of poker, a throwback to my free-as-air days of twenty years ago.

All these activities kept me from being a father to my children, and after a few months I became bored and unhappy with myself. My kids began to seem remote. My youngest would not stay overnight in my apartment and the other two, while still affectionate, were beginning to exclude me from their lives. After one long week of work, a dinner party, an all-night poker game and a few superficial dates, I decided that my family was more interesting. Life without regular involvement with my kids seemed like slow poisoning. I didn't seek a cure, although I couldn't rid myself of a peculiar, something-is-not-right feeling. One day the light bulb appeared over my head and I started to be with my kids regularly. The peculiar feeling then subsided.

# 4
## *Putting the Family First*

## HOW OFTEN DO YOU SEE YOUR KIDS?

We struck up a conversation with another middle-aged man at a local bar. He overheard us discussing divorce and wanted to talk. After the introduction, he—an office manager from a Boston suburb—revealed his divorced dad problems. The topic excited him. His digital watch and cigarette tip glowed as he punctuated the air with one hand and cut through the accumulated smoke with the other. With hands circling and slicing, he got right to the heart of the matter.

"You guys divorced too? I've got two kids and it's really tough. I'm just recovering from another bout with my ex-wife." (He lifted his scotch and water in a mock toast, either to her or to their recent bout.) "Last month she didn't want the kids to stay overnight because I had a woman living with me. A few days ago the woman moved out, and my wife said the kids shouldn't stay because there wasn't a woman around. Jesus! Ya can't win."

Without knowing us, he figured we would be sympathetic. Call it birds of a feather or even male chauvinism; it is always there when you meet a divorced dad. You can get right into a serious conversation without a lot of warmup. This conversation followed the usual pattern. It began with complaints about the former wife and ended with a not-quite-candid discussion about the kids.

"How much time do you get to see your kids?" one of us asked.

"Every weekend, at least one of the days. Sometimes it's Saturday and sometimes Sunday."

"You see them at least four or five times a month?"

"Yeah, it usually works out that way, unless there's a holiday or I have to be out of town, which is about once a month. Then I don't make it once a week. Also, sometimes, it just isn't convenient. Like I mentioned a minute ago, my ex-wife hasn't been letting the kids stay over lately, so it's been rough trying to see them."

To be sure, you can't find all of life's truths in casual bar conversations, but that one accurately reflects how most divorced dads we know operate. Most are less than candid about the amount of time they actually spend with their kids. In the early stages of divorce we were the same way.

When queried by a friend or relative we would stretch the truth a bit. It usually went something like this: "How you doin' since the divorce?" followed by a general question about the kids (their health and school progress). And then they moved quickly to the question they wanted to ask first but couldn't: "Do you spend much time with your kids?"

Without missing a beat, we would say "Oh, sure" and then steer the conversation away from the topic which hit us the hardest. If you were involved every day with your kids as a married father, you will feel bad about no longer living with them. You know they need a lot of time with you in order to become whole people, so instead of being honest about the amount of time you spend with them, you answer the question with how you would like it to be instead of how it really is.

Only a divorced dad knows how hard it is to get his former wife, his kids, and his fathering impulses synchronized. Even when you get them flowing together, the confluence is often interrupted by a catastrophe—snow storms, floods, or emergencies at the office. You solve the catastrophe by setting another time to see your children, and that can often become another problem instead of the solution anticipated. The gap between your goals and reality widens. Saying that you see your kids regularly doesn't make it so, despite all your best intentions.

If you are feeling bad about how little time you are with your children, there are several things you must do. First, you have to get rid of any residue of guilt. Then you have to examine how much time you *really* spend. Do this by writing down the lapsed time between pick-up and delivery. Be straight about it. Chances are that it will come to about three hours once or twice a week. If they have been good hours—you talked and listened and did not have any other adults or kids around vying for your attention—then six hours a week of intensive being together is not bad. Compare those quality hours with this: a number of national surveys have shown that most middle-class fathers of preschool children spend only five minutes a day interacting with their kids. Those same children in a married household watch TV about four hours, are with their moms about six, and spend the rest of the time in play and sleep. But only five minutes with their married, in-house dad! So, even though you don't live with your kids, don't automatically feel guilty or assume that a married father would be spending more time with them. Make sure that whatever time you do spend is quality time. If it is, both you and your children will want to find a way to be together more.

The way to get more regular involvement is to plan beyond the six hours. This means arranging to have them with you more in your home. The thought of another schedule or system in addition to your job, the court decree and your social life may seem odious, but it is the only way to beat feeling guilty when you tell people you spend "a lot of time" with your kids.

A child-sharing plan provides predictability for you, your children, and your former wife. You'll be able to recreate the day-to-day activities you shared with your kids during marriage. They need routine. They need to be able to predict when you will be with them and what it will be like. The amount of time, the conditions, and the way the plan develops depend on your lifestyle. It will be one of the most important things you do in your life, so we recommend that you do it cautiously and with the help of your kids. You don't have to rush out this very moment and devise a plan. On the contrary, the child-sharing plan should be evolutionary and flexible. It will take time. After a few years ours are still developing and changing. But they are working.

## THE SHEPARD CHILD-SHARING PLAN

Creating a routine for my kids grew out of a bad experience. Aaron, age five, the youngest of three children, had finally agreed to spend the night with me. His two older sisters had already done so. They reported to their brother that they had fun—they got to stay up late and ate some unusual food. However, Aaron was not taken by the prospect of leaving his mother. He still blamed himself and me for the divorce and was unsure of himself *sans* mother.

When lured with tales of late-night excitement and exotic food, he agreed. The three kids arrived, deposited their overnight gear, and we all sat together on the front porch before dinner on a beautiful summer evening. The dinner was less than exotic, but it was a change from their mother's well-prepared meals. Afterwards came fun and card games, but as bedtime loomed, so did Aaron's belief that he wanted his mother. While at that time it was hard for me to think about anyone other than myself, I did sense Aaron's gloom and anxiety.

I had mixed emotions. I first felt that he should "tough it out." This was replaced by, "Let the little shit go home." Finally I followed his sisters' suggestions that we should contact their mother. She was called and agreed to retrieve him. I extracted a semi-promise that Aaron would try an overnight again . . . soon. And he did. Had I pushed it and not notified his mother, Aaron's fear and distrust might have taken longer to overcome.

Aaron, albeit a small person, had large fears about what life would be like away from his mother overnight, and it took me a while to realize what he was going through. On my part, I squeaked through the episode because one of my daughters accurately interpreted Aaron's feelings and his mother behaved decently. It would have been easy for her to make a few emotional bucks from his immediate rejection. But she didn't. And I learned a few things. The most important was: as a divorced dad, even when you feel that you are performing valiantly, you may have to switch gears. You may have to muster your best instincts, consider the kids' feelings, and be ready not to make a mountain out of a molehill.

Being rejected by Aaron caused me to start viewing

myself from my kids' perspective. When Aaron said unequivocally that he wanted his mother, an alarm went off in my brain. At first it was a personal threat. I was upset. But I began to realize it was Aaron who needed help, not me. He was the important person in that encounter and, as the parent, I had to figure out why he wanted his mom. Later I came to understand that he thought I was like the Lone Ranger—always disappearing after performing some derring-do feat—admired and loved, but not always reliable. The only difference after his first attempt at staying overnight was that he now knew where I lived.

When the emotional dust settled, I realized more than ever that I needed to regularize my relationship with my kids. Without discussing it much I became more availabe. It is hard for me to remember exactly how I changed or how long it took me to get from episodic involvement to a regular child-sharing plan, since it is not a time in my life that I'm particularly proud of. But I believe it started the next week when my former wife phoned to say she was going to the West Coast on business. I volunteered to take a few days off work and take care of the kids.

At the time it seemed like a big leap. None of us were sure how this was going to work. They came to my almost barren apartment and we went through what was to be the oft-repeated exercise of getting unpacked. Aaron seemed a little relieved. He knew that his mom was flying across the country and that his dad was going to be the *only* parent for the next few days. He was, after a few muffled sobs into his stuffed animal that night, ready to sleep at his dad's "house." It worked! We began to enjoy the first few days of having to face each other at breakfast, lunch and dinner without buffers or outs. These were giant steps for all of us, but we began to discover new ways of being with each other. They became not just kids, but people with points of view and personalities which demanded my involvement.

When my former wife returned, the kids were glad to see her. They said they had a good time and wanted to do it again. They had survived without their mom; that was progress. After this round we went from one-night visits to two-night visits, over the weekend. Sometimes the visit began on Friday, sometimes on Saturday. In the latter instance I had to pack lunches on Monday morning and take the kids to school in their mother's town, a few minutes' drive from my apartment. Doing that made me realize that these were some of the moments I didn't want to miss: early morning discussions about what their day would be like, and seeing their friends greet them at the school door. Weekend visiting was fine, but the kids and I sensed that there could and should be more.

Thus our child-sharing arrangement grew step by step. Slowly at first, because I had no one to share my experiences with and no models to imitate, I began to figure out how I could be a real dad (as I had been in marriage). There was a lot of trial and error. And, as parents know, your kids rarely thank you when they are pleased. You wonder if you're doing right by them. It was especially hard to get accurate feedback from the kids because they were still not sure about what was going to happen. I had gone through a few months of not communicating except superficially, so they wouldn't really tell me how they liked or disliked the new schedule.

I became unsure about the effect my active participation had on my kids and backed off a bit. Quickly, however, they told both their mother and me that they wanted their dad involved in their lives in a major way. They approached each parent separately and asked them to discuss it together. At that point child sharing was quickly made formal.

After the regular weekend schedule had begun and things seemed to be working well, we began to backslide. I continued to try to keep up with my usual work and social life patterns, and for a while we almost lost the growing predictability and good feeling we had just established. But then the kids spoke up again. And their question, "Where have you been? We expected to be with you last weekend!" could not be answered merely with good intentions, a Disneyland Dad event, or a Big Mac.

The child-sharing plan became part of the contract/separation agreement that my former wife and I wrote. From the first she wanted sole custody, and I knew to fight it in court would prolong what is never an era of good feelings. But the separation contract was my former wife's and my attempt to get our thoughts straight before society, in the form of the courts, intervened. Ultimately it became part of the divorce agreement, even though my former wife wanted and got sole custody. The separation agreement and the divorce decree stated that the kids were to spend up to 50% of their time with their father and that he would be solely responsible for their well-being during those times.

But a formal agreement is one thing; real life is another. How does one establish a pattern that will satisfy everyone? Our formal arrangement began by setting a schedule of five days at Mom's, followed by three or four days at Dad's. This proved unsatisfactory for several reasons. The first was that my former wife and I had to negotiate and work out the plans before each time period (our jobs both had unusual travel requirements). Thus the children did not know until the last minute where they were to spend the next several days. Second, we discovered that five days were too long to be away from one parent. Too often the new schedule proved exhausting, not helpful.

A calendar proved to be the missing ingredient, adding predictable, predetermined times and regular visits to child sharing. Each January 1 two large desk size calendars are filled in. One of the kids gets different colored magic markers and writes an "M" or a "D" (representing Mom's or Dad's house) on each day of every month. A calendar then goes to both homes. A month's plan looks like this:

| S | M | T | W | T | F | S |
|---|---|---|---|---|---|---|
|   | D | M | M | M | D | D |
| D | M | D | D | D | M | M |
| M | D | M | M | M | D | D |
| D | M | D | D | D | M | M |
| M | D | M |   |   |   |   |

The children spend one day with their dad, three with their mother, then three with their dad and one with their mother. Weekends alternate between their dad and mother. The only exception to the pattern is when one of the parents has to be out of town; in that case days are traded. But the children know where they will be and when. They can invite their friends for an overnight. They can plan their holidays and birthdays. The kids look at the two calendars in each of their homes often. They use them to plan special events; so do their parents. The advent of a system actually enables everyone to be *more* flexible. Without it the flexibility you think you'll achieve turns to chaos. No one benefits from randomness, *particularly not kids of divorced parents*.

Our schedule is not set in concrete—either parent can ask for a change. On the other hand, parents and children plan around it; it is a fulcrum for all their activities. In its own way the schedule helps parents organize their work and social life around their children rather than fitting their children into the gaps in time not taken up by work and other events. For example, appointments for out-of-town work, if not absolutely tied to a specific time, can be planned with the schedule in mind. Usually work out of town is not planned three months in advance. Instead, someone will call and say, "We want to meet with you at our office in Dayton to discuss the report you submitted. When can you do it?" You know you are due to have your kids during the first part of next week, so you establish the meeting for Thursday. Without the schedule you'd make a time and then phone your former wife to ask her to take the kids, only to find that she was planning to be out of town on the same day. After an unpleasant conversation, during which you proclaim that without your work there'd be no support payments, you lose a small part of the good feelings and trust which you've been building. The result? You don't see your kids for several weeks.

This sort of logistical haggling can be exhausting for everyone. That is why a longterm schedule makes sense. However, we have been child sharing for approximately three years. The calendar didn't happen overnight; it took almost two years of gestation. It took time and effort to get to this point, and things may change as the kids become teenagers.

## THE GOLDMAN FAMILY ROUTINE

I have been divorced the second time for about a year. My child-sharing arrangements are not nearly as well formed as are the Shepards'. Their's is a full-blown "mature" plan. While my former wife and I agree on the importance of sharing our children, we're still groping for the right balance for all of us. As our child-sharing plan develops it probably will not become a carbon copy of the Shepards'. Our lives are different. Whatever plan you work out will differ from each of ours for this same reason.

My former wife moved from the house we shared to another town about fifteen miles away. This means that when my kids visit me they return to their old home and room. They can play with old friends and do familiar things. They have little adjustment to make to me in my environment. Their adjustment has been to their new place. For this reason, as well as because my work requires considerable travel during the week, I don't share my kids fifty-fifty with my former wife. It has been important that they adjust to their new home and that means spending time there: after-school time, weekend time, vacation time.

I usually have them for one or two nights each week. When we separated my former wife and I had a general understanding that the children would alternate weekends with each parent. However, given the difficulties which a single parent has in raising children, earning money, and maintaining some form of adult social life, there have been opportunities for me to take some of the pressure off my former wife by being with the kids at least some part of each week. Both of us now count on this, within the framework of alternate weekends.

Here's an example. I usually work at home on Fridays. One Friday, the start of a non-visiting weekend for me, I awoke to a medium-heavy snowstorm. Turning on the early news I heard that schools would be closed. Since my former wife has to be at her job at 8:45 A.M., I knew that she would be trying to hustle up a babysitter. I phoned her to tell her that I would take the kids. There was a big sigh of relief on the other end of the phone. Could I take them for the whole day? She had to get her car fixed in the late afternoon. We decided that I would keep them overnight and return them early on Saturday morning.

My former wife and I have no schedule or written plan. She knows when my time is likely to be flexible each week. Usually there is some need for me to help with the kids during those times. The phone calls between us to set this up are more than either of us would like. But even these are becoming fewer and more productive as each parent becomes better at interpreting the other's usual weekly activities. Some type of formal plan will evolve as the months pass. We both want to reach that point because to reach it will provide each of us with more time to pursue our individual lives, and better time to be with our kids.

## DEVELOPING YOUR OWN SOLUTION

"Horse sense" was the missing ingredient in her father's relationship to her brother, said writer Brooke Hayward in answer to a query about what went wrong with that now famous family. With all the Haywards' inherent talent, richness, and cultural and educational opportunities, their father's lack of common sense led to results which have been well chronicled in her book *Haywire*. Horse sense too often is a missing ingredient in divorced dads' relationships to their kids. We believe that most of what we have to say in this section is more related to horse sense than any other skill. Using your head about your kids in their new role with you as a divorced dad is one of the most difficult things you will do during the early stages.

It is obvious that a child-sharing plan has to consist of more than days colored in on a calendar, or a genral agreement that the kids will be with one or the other parent every weekend. To be effective a plan calls for trust and flexibility and must encompass everyone's ideas—including the kids'. We talk to our children and former wives about how well they think things are work-ing and ask, periodically, if anyone wants any changes. However, thus far the days marked on the calendar seem to have been the single most important part of beginning a plan for the Shepard family. For the Goldmans it is the alternate weekends and the flexibility which seems to be important.

In additon to schedules, there are several other less tangible aspects of child sharing. First of all you must keep tension and hostility low during difficult times. Remember that the important thing is to keep you and your children together. With that in mind, try to be tolerant.

Say you arrive at your former wife's house to get your children. You had a hard day at the office. You know there are several traffic jams to get through in the next few minutes. You know that when you get to your house, late and tired, you will have to unpack the car and then fix dinner. Unless you have the serenity of Buddha you will be upset when your former wife tells you that the kids are not ready. That *she* has had a hard day. That the clothes for their visit are in the dryer. That the kids' gloves are wet because they were playing in the snow until a few minutes ago. That you and she have a few things to talk about.

At moments like this you will feel like giving her and maybe even the kids a few choice words. Not only are the kids not ready, but (you find out) one of them has been giving your former wife a hard time. She wants you to give the kid a character guidance lecture when you get to your house. Then she hands you the dentist bills. You peruse them quickly. Trying to avoid losing your cool but feeling compelled to say something, you ask, "I thought they had really good teeth with all that fluoride they get?" Your former wife may or may not take this the right way, but she responds, "They do have good teeth—*those* bills are just for cleaning and a checkup."

If it is important to you to enjoy the next few days with your kids, be tolerant. You have to avoid the way you might have behaved when you were married. If the same scene had been played when you were living with your former wife and kids you would have been able to use the rising costs of dentistry as an excuse to get angry.

The same anger will not work now that you are a divorced dad. If you allow yourself to vent your anger and anxiety, you'd leave your former wife's house in a snit, trailing the kids behind. They will wonder what the two of you were yelling about, and when you get to your house you will start their time with you on a somber note. And it may be days or weeks before the air is cleared.

Resist the urge to air your feelings then and there; wait for a more suitable time to go over the highly charged issues. If a child-sharing plan is going to work, it will require that you and your former wife have a lot more interaction than either of you may like. The tension between you, which wanes with each succeeding year of divorce, is always present in some form when you have contact. You want that tension to affect your children as little as possible. Finances, in-laws or other mates may be sources of irritation. They are your problems and they need not burden your children. If you must go over them, pick a time when your kids are not likely to be present. As hard as it may be, try to keep these and similar issues out of bounds when you and your former wife are with your youngsters.

We are not saying that anger between two former spouses should be hidden from their children. The kids are aware of it. They've heard it before. If there is tension or hostility between their parents during picking-up and dropping-off times, the kids will sense it. But why assault them with battles which are not of their making, and about which they can do nothing? If you want your kids to gain all that is possible from your involvement with them, try to keep the increased interaction with your former wife free of hostility.

A second rule to keep in mind is the need for trust. You must be where you say you will be, and on time. And you must be sure the children are where they are supposed to be during the times you are the responsible parent. When you all lived together there was one home base to touch. You could afford to be a little late. Everyone showed up at the house sooner or later. But now there are two houses. And you don't want to turn your child sharing into an Abbott and Costello "Who's on First?" routine.

It should be clear that your active role in your kids' lives will be most effective when they feel secure about you. You build security not only through letting them know that you love them, but by being predictable. This means sticking to the letter of any arrangements. It also requires a contingency plan if you are unavoidably detained.

Here's an example. When the Goldmans first separated, the former wife had an appointment out of town. She told the children (ages six and eight at the time) that their dad would pick them up at school and they would stay with him for several days. Allowing just enough time to meet them at the end of their day, he started out and had a flat tire on a back road far from a phone. Changing the tire meant he was twenty minutes late. The kids were starting a new school and were living in a new place. They knew their mother was not at home. As their dad drove toward their school he feared for what they might be feeling: scared in a new place and neither parent there. He was also uncertain where to look for them once he got there. Would they be at the school or at home?

Driving to the school he found them sitting on the playground swings. He hugged them and asked if they had been upset or worried. They reminded him that he had told them the previous week to wait at the appointed place if he was ever late. He had said, "Stay where I'm supposed to meet you. That will be the first place I look if I'm delayed." They also replied they were sure he would be along very soon. This worked for the Goldman children and is a good rule for your kids, given the logistical problems involved in all child-sharing plans. Develop a contingency plan in case you are unavoidably late sometime.

All manner of events can combine to upset a predictable routine. The weather is bound to, especially if you and your former wife do not live within easy distance of each other. Rain and snow will slow you down, tire you out, and disrupt your plane schedule. Sometimes you will feel as if you have to mount the Normandy invasion just to see your child. Anton Goldman and his dad have a standing joke about how it "always" snows when they are to get together. The classic time which they will always remember was when Anton was five. His dad drove alone, to Anton's mother's home on roads of sheet ice. It took three hours to go sixty-five miles. After Anton was picked up, their car hit a skid. They were pulled out of a snowbank with a four-wheel-drive vehicle, but not before they waited in the car on a lonely road for what seemed an eternity. Anton was returned to his mother in the four-wheel-drive. After dropping him off, his dad crept away to a motel.

That was not an isolated incident. Keeping a consistent pattern of contact with Anton has been hard and exhausting at times. During the winter their time together has been resheduled about 50% of the time. Anton has learned to accept it.

If there is considerable geographic distance between you and your former wife, you will not always be in control of the child-sharing schedule. Fighting the weather or taking public transportation with all its delays is tiring and frustrating. You are not as alert and excited by the time you see your kid. Then you have to explain the reasons for being late or your change in plans to your kids and to your ex-wife. You should help the kids understand what causes you to alter your plans and inform them what you expect them to do when you are late.

With only one child the picking-up and dropping-off process is relatively simple once each parent feels confident that the other will act according to plan. When there are several children of varying ages, however, picking up and dropping off can be confusing and time consuming. Consider this scenario. When you arrive to pick up the kids, you discover one is at a birthday party, one has a violin lesson, and the third is at the dentist. You become overwhelmed. How can you collect them, check their clothes, and move them to your place without devoting a whole day to it? Well, if you and your ex-wife are cooperating with each other, she will have given them instructions about exactly where you will meet each of them. They will also take this seriously because they're aware that shortening the picking-up process depends on their effort as well. The bags are packed and ready before they leave for their appointments. At the most you have four stops (one for the bags) and, if everyone understands what time they will be met, the process need not be confusing.

Up to this point we have been talking about a particular kind of trust—the belief that you will be where you agreed to be at about the right time. Now we would like to get you to think about trust in relation to your former wife.

## KEEPING YOUR BARGAINS

If you can't agree on some fundamental things with your former wife, your child sharing plan—no matter how modest—will not work. We do not need to say anthing about how hard it is even to talk with a former wife, especially just after separation or divorce. There are hundreds of dramatic stories which relate that. We know it is hard, but you have to develop a way of dealing with her so that you can get yourself and your kids together.

The most important thing you will have to do with her is to make sure that you keep your bargains. You must also keep schedules for picking up the kids and for paying whatever you have agreed to pay her. You have to be better about the schedules than you were when you were married. If you think you will not get there in time to pick up the kids, then call.

Why is it important to make sure that you keep to schedules? If you don't, then both your children and former wife have reason to complain. Your kids are concerned that you don't love them as you did when you were around full time. Your former wife can indeed, if so inclined, get some mileage out of the fact that you were not interested enough in seeing your kids to get there on time. Adherence to schedule should also apply when you deliver them back to their mother's house. Both you and your former wife have to act as though the schedule were a business arrangement. You agreed to pick up the children at 5:30 and to return them a few days later at 9:00, and you should not be more than 15 minutes late in either direction.

Apart from keeping your bargains and adhering to schedules as a way to lower anxiety and hostility, there is at least one other reason. Children (indeed, most human beings) have a built-in energy clock. They will adjust their emotions and actions according to their ex-

46

pectations of when an event is going to begin or end. If that event is off schedule by very much, then you will probably have missed the "magic moment" and have several out-of-phase children on your hands.

Being on time may sound like a pretty small issue, but remember that it is the small issues that will start you on the right path to being an involved divorced father. When you are on time the kids do not have to sit with their snowsuits on in an overheated room (your former wife always kept the house too hot, right?). If you are late and your former wife has made plans to do something other than stay at home when you picked up the children, it will mess up her plans. Also remember that when the kids are waiting for you in their full regalia with their clothes all packed and ready, your former wife will have to provide a lot of discussion about why you are not there. Chances are that they will give their mother a harder time about their father not being on time than they will you—the man in their lives who is going to take them out to do something interesting. So if you are more that 15 minutes late, everyone will probably be upset and you will have to start your time with your children having just had another difficult moment with their mother. Also, being on time will probably throw her off balance. She, given that you have just missed a child support or house payment, thinks you are chaotic and that your lateness is the evidence. If you are on time, however, not early or late, then the wind is taken from her sails. All in all, promptness means that you and your kids will be able to start your time together in a good mood.

There is also a political reason for being on time or keeping your word about things you have agreed to do. That is simply that a child-sharing plan, as it matures, will require a great deal of flexibility on everyone's part. This means that down the road you will all have to make a number of allowances. But you shouldn't start off that way. If you are punctual—with payments and pick-up times—you will be able to build up some goodwill for when there is a real need for flexibility and understanding.

Initially it is hard to remember that you are no longer married; even if she was somewhat sympathetic before, she surely has little or no reason to be so now, unless you start scoring a few points. It is difficult to remember that even though you still see and deal with this person, times have changed. You have to build a new relationship with new rules and new patterns, and that is damned difficult.

## VACATIONS, HOLIDAYS, BIRTHDAYS

Good childhood memories warm and comfort us in later life when the going gets cold and hard. Invariably these memories are linked with family: Christmas morning, a Labor Day picnic, an overnight trip to the ocean or city. You can still give these times to your kids—secure, vivid memories they will hold onto for the rest of their lives. You can create them yourself, just for you and your kids. Or you can share them with your former wife by extending, a little bit, the contact which you have with each other already.

The reality is that you both share your kids. You talk about them probably more than either of you thought you would. Sharing your children is probably the least painful part of the divorce. Why stop doing that entirely when you, your former wife, and the kids can all benefit by it?

You need not do it frequently or routinely, but your children might benefit from periodic family events. These can range from a meal together at one parent's place or a pizza at a local restaurant. Or they can be quiet conversations among parents and kids, a game of Monopoly in which everyone participates, or even a picnic at the beach.

You can use these opportunities to satisfy any residual Disneyland Dad inclinations which you might have. And given the likelihood that you and your former wife had serious interpersonal problems in the past, sharing an event which minimizes heavy personal interaction may be best.

Keep your kids' best interest in mind. If a shared activity appears to be the least bit awkward, don't do it. If you or your former wife are committed in any way to another person, it will be increasingly difficult for you to organize even brief shared times. And the complexity which other individual sensitivities add to the situation may prohibit your considering the plan at all.

Once you've resolved in your mind the problems we've raised, as well as specific issues pertaining only to your circumstances, call a cease-fire with your former wife for a day or a few hours. Agree that you'll spend a prescribed time together with your kids. Call all the sore spots (support payments, personal discussions, etc.) out of bounds. You will then participate in one of the least complex and purely altruistic aspects of family life—parents sharing the joy of being with their kids. You don't have to abandon that totally because you've divorced.

Be aware that this may not work all the time, or for every family. If you have any doubts that you and your former wife can carry it off, don't try it.

While we're dealing with thorny issues, we should mention the problem of birthdays (yours, your former wife's, and the kids'). Here we really don't have a lot of advice, except to say that a straightforward discussion with the rest of the family will help.

In the Shepard family divorce was the framework in which the father discovered he liked planning and giving birthday parties (a bit of the Disneyland Dad in us all). The former wife did not. Thus she quickly relinquished two of the three children's birthday parties. For holidays, the Shepards generally divide them so that each year Thanksgiving and Christmas are spent in different homes, and the kids generally manage to have two Christmases (which, for the moment, is one of the few added attractions their married-family-peers don't have). Holidays are indeed difficult times and there are several other arrangements. The Goldman family has rejoined at Christmas for at least two years, but the Shepards have alternated holidays from one year to the next.

Now, what about presents? Given that all our children are preteenagers, it is difficult for them to amass enough money to be able to buy gifts for their parents. Thus former wives contribute to Fathers' Day, birthday and Christmas gifts for their divorced husband. The same goes for the dad. There is nothing complex here. It will happen, and the kids will expect that both parents will act generously.


## BEDROOMS AND TEDDY BEARS

If you had to set up your own place after the separation, you know how stark and bare it can be. In the first months your paycheck doesn't even seem to cover the financial arrangements you made with your former wife, so furnishing your new home in any complete way is out of the question for the moment. All you have is a bed, a TV, a table and chair. It is hard to feel civilized and harder still to visualize a life which includes more than a few hours a week visit with your kids. You don't want to bring them to your place because there's nothing for them to do there, and the whole scene depresses both you and them.

In time, as your new life solidifies, you'll establish more permanent, comfortable surroundings. As you do you'll have to think about providing a place for your youngsters there if you want to be active in their lives. However small or large your accommodations, your kids need a part of it that is permanently theirs. You needn't rush out and furnish it all at once. In fact a gradual approach which involves your children is best. Each of us was separated for over a year before we bought dressers for our children. Other pressing financial demands kept us from doing so. So did motivation or access to a furniture store. Finally, when we each bought bedroom furniture for our kids, they loved it and made a big thing out of unpacking their bags and putting away their clothes.

Creating a special place for your children means helping them feel secure and comfortable there. Without those feelings as a base, you'll have difficulty developing the closeness that you all want and need. Your goal is to create an environment, or system, which enables all of you to be yourselves, naturally.

The system has two major parts. The first is comprised of the special possessions to which the children are attached and which give them a sense of permanence in your home. The second includes all the regular essentials which, if they have them at your place, will minimize a lot of packing back and forth from mom's house.

The special possessions will vary according to the children's ages and interests. For younger kids it may be several stuffed animals, a favorite blanket, or a special toy; for older kids, sports equipment or books. Whatever these items are, their permanence at your place will help the kids establish a sense of permanence in their lives.

You can't move children around like Patton moved

the Fifth Army. You can't expect them to get to your house with a complete set of everything, even when you pick them up and pack for them at their mom's house. Invariably you'll realize that someone has only one sock or no undershirt. Therefore, it's best to obtain some essentials which are always at your house. Either the kids won't ever have to pack them, or they will know you have a spare if they forget. The two basics are a set of spare clothing and toilet articles, especially toothbrushes.

With a system, your time together will be less clouded by your kids feeling like guests. The goal is to help them feel they have two permanent homes.

Being without certain clothing can hamper any activities you may have planned. For example, you can pick up your kids on a beautiful sunny day and find them ready and all packed. But the next day turns out rainy and you realize that no one thought to bring a raincoat. One way of avoiding this is to make a ritual of packing by listing all the things they are likely to need and going over the list before leaving their mom's house. As stated several times in these pages, kids love rituals. If you get them small colorful dufflebags and set up the packing ritual, you'll find that problems of missing clothing, which can detract from your time together, will occur less and less often. Your children will develop a greater sense of responsibility for their things when they see how necessary keeping track is.

But maybe my kid should have two raincoats, you say. That's a possibility. If you have the means and the time, you could outfit him completely with a separate wardrobe at each house. Neither of us has used this approach, although we both share some of the clothes buying with our former wives. Putting aside the cash factor, two complete wardrobes is not only a duplication of effort but can consume an enormous amount of time as you update growing children's clothing. Besides, if the children carry some major personal belongings with them, they are likely to feel more secure at your place. Keep some spare socks, some underwear, a shirt, a sweater, and a pair of jeans on hand. That should do it.

Having your children clean up their room before you take them back is also important. If you develop a system where this is done right before leaving your place, you'll ensure their return with all the things your former wife depends on to care for them properly. She can't make do with one shoe either.

The two Goldman daughters have never been famous for being neat and orderly. One day as they were about to leave and father and daughters were all clowning around, their father yelled to them in their room in a drill sergeant's voice that he was coming up to inspect. He shouted that they'd better have their room neat and be standing at attention by their beds. When he got there they were at attention, barely suppressing giggles, but with their bags packed and the room neater than it had ever been. To his surprise they loved the inspection routine, loved the pretend possibility of some unknown but terrible punishment. Now they do it every time they leave for their mom's house. Their room is always neat when they leave and their belongings are well packed. In six months they've cut the packing and clean-up time down to about three minutes.

If you share your children on a regular basis you'll have to have a place for them to sleep. We can't tell you a rock-bottom, dirt-cheap way of resolving the bedding issue. There probably isn't one. Remember that bedtime is an important time in a young child's day. You can tell how secure your kids feel when you kiss them goodnight. If they miss their mother or are troubled in some way, you'll know about it then. While you don't have to provide a Louis XV four poster with canopy, a cozy bed in a cozy corner adds to the secure feeling. Some thought about what the bed and bedding should be like for your kids is very important.

There are ways of making inexpensive bed frames from plywood. A how-to-do-it book on mobile furniture will give you ideas. Sheets can be a drag because of the time and effort required to keep them clean. There are colorful indoor sleeping bags on the market which are relatively inexpensive. They need periodic cleaning but not the constant washing that sheets do. And they're easier to straighten out than making a bed.

To round out your kids' place, there should be the usual child equipment: games, toys, art supplies. In the beginning, when the place is bare, you can go shopping together and stock up. Doing it gradually will create continuing activities for you to share. Obtaining all these things on your own and at once, even if you have the means to do it, eliminates the possibilities for planning together, shopping together, and choosing together.

Finally, you and the kids can make some of the furniture if the space and your inclinations allow. A box to keep toys in is a good start. Putting up shelves instead of a bureau is an alternative. Making a bureau or clothes rack are other possibilities.

## YOUR KIDS AND THEIR FRIENDS

Your children will feel at home in your house when they become familiar with the neighborhood, and particularly the other kids. You may have to help them establish new relationships. There are active and passive approaches to this. In the latter instance, you can be outside with your kids during every opportunity the weather will allow. Throw a ball, start to play a game with them and, like bears to honey, when there is a dad playing with his children, other kids will appear. Obviously you then ask them to join you, and bingo! Your children have some friends. The active mode requires a little more effort. When one of your kids has a birthday, ring a few doorbells and ask to have some of the neighborhood children over for a small party. This works. At the slightest mention of a birthday party, you will find those you previously saw with dirty faces and running noses will appear at your door on time, clean, and excited. (You've got to be careful here and make sure that you will recognize them in their cleaned-up state.) The reason a birthday party is a good way for your kids to meet others is obvious. All children love birthday parties. The neighborhood kids will bring presents (no matter how firmly you tell them not to.). They do this not so much to prove they have big hearts, but because they know they have expanded their own gift-receiving possibilities when *their* birthday arrives. You may think that your neighbors are stand-offish, but they become much less so when you invite their child to a party. The invitation makes both the parent and the kid happy. You become some parent's free babysitter for a few hours, and the kid is looking forward to all the goodies.

There may be some parents, however, who are reluctant to have their kids become overly involved with the children of a divorced father. It happened to the Shepards.

When friends of the Shepard girls had been invited to a birthday party at their dad's apartment, some of their peers' mothers were hesitant. The girls broached the subject with their dad. "Mona Stephens can't come 'cuz her mom doesn't know where you live." Mona Stephens had played at the Shepard girls' mother's home frequently, and in fact had stayed overnight on a number of occasions. The Shepard dad remembered that Mona was not always picked up on time, and that Mona's mother was not concerned enough to check out the Shepard mother's house before allowing her daughter to stay overnight. Yet, when merely invited to an afternoon lawn birthday party, Mona could not attend.

The Shepard father's impulse was to tell his daughter that her mother's friend should "stick it in her ear." His next impulse was to out-maneuver Mona's mom. How to do it?

Since the birthday was a few days away, he calmly told his daughter not to worry. He then planned for an assault on Mona's mom's middle-class "anti-divorced dad" prejudices. In a day or so, he drove to Mona's house. Before anyone could erect any more prejudicial barriers, he was in Mona's house, dazzling her mom with his responsible adult, statesman, good-guy, lover-of-children routine.

"Hi, Mrs. Stephens. I wanted to make sure Mona could come to Holly's birthday. She's Holly's best friend, so we want to make sure she can come."

Mrs. Stephens was off guard. Making nervous little gestures with her hands, she said, "Well, I wasn't sure who was going to be there, or how long the party would last."

Without missing a beat and loving the opportunity to display another virtue (good organizing skills), the Shepard dad launched into the whole schedule. "Well, we are going to be on the lawn of my Watertown house (a slight lie—it was a two-family structure). I've hired a mime and a band of students who've been performing in Harvard Square. It will be exciting, and you should stay awhile after you drop Mona off. Here's a map and my phone number."

Mona's mom, flustered as she was, could not refuse face-to-face. "Okay, I'll drop her off and pick her up."

Holly was delighted and, while there were other times when having a divorced dad for a father would cause each of the Shepard kids some discomfort, they felt after that performance that their dad could pass inspection by any person who was hesitant and overly concerned about the morals or accountability of divorced dads. There have been other episodes, however, in which the kids were made to feel uncomfortable about having divorced parents and especially a divorced dad. Peers and parents often have strong prejudices. Why? We are not sure. Possibly many parents have bought the "swinging divorced dad" stereotype and believe that having their kids around children whose parents have been divorced will expose them to the disease. We doubt that such an epidemiological explanation is worth pursuing.

You should ask your kids from time to time about their peers' perception of your family arrangements. If you ask, you can often stop any real problems in the early stages.


## YOU AND YOUR KIDS

The Shepard and Goldman child-sharing plans help keep us from being Disneyland Dads. For a variety of reasons each system is different. The Shepard plan, aged and mellowing, has developed over a longer time period. Yet both of us are with our children for a significant amount of time, as real people and as parents.

What sort of arrangement should you have? That depends. The glue that holds a child-sharing plan together is the parents' willingness to share the children and not compete for them. This means that both parents have to be responsible and responsive to each other, even if only where their kids are concerned.

Initially it is not the calendar or some other artifice which will make the plan work. It is direct, serious discussion with your former wife and your kids (at their level of understanding) about all of your reasons for being with them. The calendars in the Shepard homes are merely a manifestation of a system that has been devised and agreed upon by the participants.

It's important that you enable your kids to participate in the process as much as possible. It may help them understand that divorce need not continue to be a battleground when they see you and your former wife talking constructively about their welfare. To the degree that they are included in the planning, they will be better able to cope with living in two homes.

In the beginning it will not matter how many days a month you are with your kids in your home doing real things. But you should have some type of system whereby everyone knows what to expect. You may start out with a few hours or days, but be prepared to expand the time as your newly devised system starts to work well.

Some adults never really like kids—their own or anyone else's. Be honest with yourself. If this is you, don't exacerbate the situation with systems and regimes that don't make anyone happy. But if you truly like your kids, then setting up a routine where you can share an occasional ordinary day can please you and can help them grow.

You may want to expand the pattern and see the kids more often, but do it slowly and carefully. Like many things in this life, it's harder to pull back after a pattern has been established then it is to establish that pattern in the first place. In fact, if you expanded your time and then wanted to pull back, it could be damaging to your children. Talk to them about what they would like. Let them in on your schedule and then negotiate with your former wife. Let her see the advantages of the plan, the most obvious one being more free time for her. Remember, you have to be flexible, even with a rigid system. Here's an example.

On those school days when you have responsibility for your kids, you will have to act responsibly. If your son becomes ill you may have to leave the most important task of the week and go retrieve him at school. You have to be prepared to take him to the doctor and then to get a babysitter or to stay home with him, at least for the rest of the day.

You were probably getting interested in our child-sharing ideas up to this point, but now you're wincing. You see only trouble. "How in hell can I explain to my boss or clients that I've got to go to school and get my son, who just tossed his cookies?" you say. It won't be easy. But think of all those working mothers who have been doing this for years, in jobs which often did not have the flexibility that yours may have. We bet that you can solve this problem. Most working mothers manage to go get their kids at school when necessary, and so can you.

This is one example of how flexible you must be. There are others, but for now think about the one we've just posed. You'll have to be prepared to make a few decisions fast. When you get to the point in your child-sharing plan where you actually do have sole responsibility for your child on a given day, you should develop a contingency plan if your kid needs you. Perhaps a neighbor can help. Even warning your boss that something like this may occur will make the problem a bit easier to handle. There is always an out. If really necessary, if all else fails, you can ask your former wife to go. But you must be ready to reciprocate and not to ask her more than once every five years or so.

It makes no sense for us to tell you how many days each month you should spend with your child. Possibly geography prohibits much interaction, and that is unfortunate. Whether the amount of time is fifty-fifty as with the Shepard kids, or less as with the Goldmans, some system with built-in flexibility is best. The models we have presented work for us, but may not work for you. The important thing to remember is that you need some sort of system. It can even be included in your divorce arrangement, but the actual way you institute it is not important. That you see your children regularly, is important.

Child sharing does mean that you will have face-to-face discussions with your former wife. You may be able to handle it, but she may feel like the female lead in *South Pacific*, who wanted to "wash that man right outta my hair" and couldn't because of the kids. This may be frustrating for both of you. Because these discussions are often marked by mixed emotions, they require statesmanship on your part. As with child-sharing itself, talking seriously with your former wife about the process need not take place all at once. Don't come on too strong too soon. The amount of child sharing, or the amount of discussion about it, is secondary to the quality of time spent with your kids and future plans made for this with your former wife.

Primarily, having a child-sharing plan means you will be totally responsible for your kids some of the time during the regular week or weekend. You can't gloss over that realization. It will mean a drastic change in your life if you have been a Disneyland Dad. Even though a child-sharing plan may alter your life as a divorced male, and may force you to develop new housekeeping skills rapidly, you have to keep in mind why you are doing it. You are sharing your kids because they need a father. They need your male presence in their lives, and you need them.

# 5

## *The Long-Distance Run*

### THE DIVORCED DAD'S MARATHON

If you are middle-aged you have probably looked in the mirror and noticed a spare tire. Your response was, no doubt, "Tomorrow I'm going to do something about this! I'm going to exercise every day. I'm going to quit drinking beer. Dammit, I'm going to get in shape." Some of us never get beyond those declarations. Others spring into action for a few days or weeks. Still others will do it right, gradually.

Being serious about reducing your beer gut means more than giving up the suds and buying a warmup suit. It calls for a fairly drastic change in your daily routine. You will have to set aside time for exercise—it has to become as automatic as brushing your teeth. Inevitably you will have to adjust your social, economic, and professional lives. In a few words, getting in shape is hard. And setting up a child-sharing arrangement of the sort we're describing will be no easier.

The child-sharing/getting-in-shape analogy is a good way to start thinking about how your life will change. However long you have been separated or divorced—a day, week, month, or even years—you need to train. Most marathon runners and sports trainers will tell you to start slowly. The first day of jogging or running or exercising is not the day to reach your goal. After all, you did not acquire the spare tire in a single day.

You cannot run the marathon before building your endurance from two miles to four, then six, and so on. You must become acquainted with your body at these distances and know when you have reached your limit. Most importantly, if you push yourself far beyond your limit you'll hurt yourself. This does no good and sets your training back for the length of time it takes your injury to heal.

Making the sacrifices which will put you actively in your kids' lives is a lot like building up the distances. Too much too early will hurt and set you back. Build up to active involvement gradually. The more time you work at it and think about it, the more involved with your kids you'll be; the longer and better you will be able to run with them. But the more time you put into it, the less free personal time you will have. To play out the analogy: Some of you may decide to become two- to four-mile runners as divorced dads. You will build up to that distance and hold steady there. Others may want to go longer distances with their kids. Personal needs, career choices, and individual personality characteristics will determine how far you go.

In order to be with your kids regularly, you will have to develop new discipline and make adjustments in at least three major areas of your life—social, economic, and professional. We alluded to some of these adjustments in the previous chapters. Here we want to share specific examples and what we think we learned.


## PLANNING A SOCIAL LIFE

Active involvement with your kids will curtail your social life. When you were married and saw the kids routinely, it wasn't a big deal to leave them for an evening with a babysitter. But it is important for you, as a beginning divorced dad, to develop a secure basis for the new life you are building with your kids. At least initially, this means staying home with them at night when they are with you.

When you create a home for them in your home, they need to know that they will find you there if they wake in the dark. This is especially important if your surroundings are unfamiliar to them, and more so if the kids are relatively young. The chances are that the events surrounding the separation were frightening and confusing for them. Being with you overnight in what is at first a strange place makes a big demand on small, and possibly perplexed, children. It will ease their minds to know that you will be there even after they go to sleep. And you can bet that at least one of your kids will wake up looking for you during the first time that they stay over.

Both of us kept close to home when our kids began staying overnight. In both families our youngest children, not yet used to being away from their mothers, would cry out at night for a parent. Our being close at hand during those times was very important. It happens less frequently now that they have tested the system and have adjusted to living in two homes. Still, we are reluctant to leave them with babysitters. If we do go out, we generally take the kids, and this means an early evening. We have time when the kids are not under our care to socialize with adults. But since we no longer see the kids every day, we tend to prefer their company when they are with us.

Not going out when the kids are with you is the first big social sacrifice you will make. Another one is including the kids when you have visitors in your home during child-sharing time. But this is not necessarily a sacrifice; your visitors may like your kids, and the serious (boring) conversation can wait till after the children's bedtime. If you ignore the kids, though, they will be unhappy. They will have good reason for their unhappiness, too. Remember, they look forward to being with you. They have to do a fair amount of planning (clothes and homework) in order to shift homes. So, when it is your time to be with them, they will usually feel great anticipation.

Consider a typical scene: You pick up the kids to drive them to your house. On the way over the chatter in the car is rapid-fire. The kids are loaded with stories. They want to tell you about what silly things their mother did. They want to tell you about school. Sometimes they have important news about their friends ("Suzie's mom and dad split"). You have to provide about fifteen minutes of your full attention. Add time for your news to them and you have about half an hour of machine gun blasts of communication.

The first half hour or so is an important time. Try not to be distracted or have other adults around them. You want to keep communication flowing with the kids, and the presence of other adults may slow it down. Try to keep this initial excitement going. Remember, it is boring to pack and unpack your clothes and other paraphernalia several times a week, so there should be a big payoff: your undivided attention. Your adult visitors can wait.

Making sure that your initial minutes with the kids are of high quality should be part of your training. Much as you would stretch your leg muscles before a two or three mile jog, devote a few undistracted minutes to your kids when you first see them.

In general we found that when we began to share our children on a regular basis, we began to be less socially active. When we did go out, it was a family night. This even carried over to vacations; we vacation in places where kids are welcome. And, for a change in scenery, we visit each other with kids. Dating, or whatever its middle-age equivalent is, deserves a section to itself.

## THE WOMEN IN YOUR LIFE

Your kids probably won't benefit if you stage Wagnerian productions of the primal scene, co-starring a different female lead every time they visit you. But short of that, how will your relationships with the grown women in your life affect your kids? We are not going to foist any parlor psychology on you. This is a complicated issue, and there are no exclusively correct answers or ways of behaving.

We have no prescriptions for exactly how a divorced dad should behave with women. Rather, we merely want you to consider what effects your behavior will have on the kids. And we both believe that the effects will be substantial. You are the model on which your children will base a lot of their feelings about the way men act in the world. If they are boys, they will emulate you. If they are girls, their responses to the men in their lives will be determined in great part by how they saw you act toward them and other women.

We realize that by taking this stand we are flying in the face of recent research by child-development experts.

The trendy research has it that kids will turn out fine even when their parents make a lot of mistakes. These recent revelations may or may not be methodologically and substantively sound. We have looked at some of the studies and we are not convinced.

The experts aside, we strongly believe that your kids need you to guide them. They need you not only as a model (passive guidance) but also as a regulator (active guidance). That is, they need you to tell them how to behave socially, professionally, and ethnically. This is not to say, by the way, that a single parent (for example, their mother) could not fill this role. She could, and hopefully does. But children need as much of this as you can provide. And, despite the jokes about Jewish mothers, no one will ever convince us that a kid ever gets too much guidance from his parents.

Now consider what has happened to your kids in their relatively short lives. They have seen the man and woman whom they love and depend on most in the world argue, bicker and separate. Probably they've heard a fair amount of hostility between their parents when you thought they were asleep. That was the scariest time, according to our kids.

If they were lucky they saw you and your former wife sharing your affection for each other when your marriage was better. They have seen you and your ex-wife in bed together, probably disturbed your lovemaking at some time, and (for sure) heard it and wondered what was going on.

So, on some level, your kids have seen and heard your very own *Scenes from a Marriage* and *Story of Adam and Eve*. They've absorbed a lot of information about how men and women get along. If they were more articulate and had a good agent, they could take business away from Harold Robbins. But they are not articulate; in fact, they probably cannot tell you what they think.

It is confusing to them. They have no perspective in which to place it. And they have only overheard fragments, since most parents try to keep both the arguing and the lovemaking outside their children's daily reality.

You have had a great deal of personal experience over the past several years. You married, fathered one or more children, and divorced. Can you pass on anything to your kids that you've learned about how men and women could or should get along? The separation and divorce have preoccupied you and the kids for a long time. Can you make the experience that you're all now living through constructive in any way?

You can and do, through your example. However, you simply cannot tell them verbally. Although you can lecture them about looking both ways before they cross the street, living with the opposite sex is a far more complicated subject. Getting hurt by a car is dramatically different from getting hurt in a relationship. The kids know that caution is the best policy when they cross the street. But with male/female relationships, caution may not always be the best policy. How can you tell that to your kids? You cannot. Passing information about men and women to your kids is done by your daily example.

Can the example you set as a divorced dad repair any damage or offset any confusion your kids may feel as the result of the divorce? Of course, they're bound to make their own mistakes in life. But your example will mould their relationships with other human beings. The baseline for children learning about how men and women interact with one another is their mother and father. This holds true for divorced as well as married couples. Obviously you do not want to criticize your former wife in front of your kids. Neither do you want to allow the children to play one parent against the other, using whatever animosity exists between them to do it. But most importantly, when you treat their mother with respect and courtesy (if you can rise above the turmoil of the divorce) you will leave a profound impression on your children.

Seeing their dad or mom in a loving involvement with another adult will help the kids learn about human relationships. A stable, realistic relationship which includes the kids can do them much good. However, many divorced parents do not remarry. An increasing number live alone and will do so for the rest of their lives. In this case, their kids will see fewer examples of the significant people in their lives sharing, loving, being part of a complete family. On the other hand they will get more attention from you and your former wife if you are not committed to a new mate. And having you exclusively to themselves can be the best possible way of putting to rest the fears and confusions felt during the divorce. They know they have all of you for as long as they need you. They will not have to share you.

The consequences of divorce on social life can vary considerably. Some divorced dads enter into a revolving-door series of sexual relationships with a wide range of women who find them attractive. Despite the pity which our culture expresses for middle-aged men as they begin the decline into senility, older men may be attractive to women of all ages. The man who has established himself in his career and has developed his abilities to deal effectively with everyday life has his appeal.

In general, out of all the people you meet in a week or a year, how many fast friends do you make, male or female? Not many. Between men and women, when a relationship has sexual possibilities (even though the two people don't actually engage in sex), and the relationship fails to grow into a more permanent or intimate friendship, it usually ends fairly quickly.

The point is, should you introduce your kids to all the women who pass through your life? When you date you may see someone once or twice and never see her again. Why confuse the kids with fleeting relationships? They have not built up their personal armor at a young age. They may take people to whom they are introduced more seriously than you do.

If your kids like a particular woman but you and she do not hit it off, for whatever reason, they will continue to ask about her long after you and she have decided not to see each other. Remember, they have just gone through a massive separation. Why stack the deck for more and needless feelings of abandonment?

We both concluded independently that we wouldn't introduce our kids to women we dated unless there were possibilities of an ongoing relationship. Moreover, we never arranged to be with a woman overnight when our kids visited. One of us has now remarried. But the rule of thumb was and is: no women in bed when the kids are around, unless there was some permanence to the relationship. There was only one reason for our behavior. Both of us decided, independently again, that the kids would be confused by introductions to people who might not be a consistent part of our lives.

Because we both reached the same conclusion does not mean that this is the only way to go. But, having reviewed in our minds what emotional adjustments the kids were struggling with during the years of separation and divorce, we decided to try to minimize their confusion. On the other hand, when one of our kids, now a preteen, realized that her dad was not introducing the children to his female friends, she asked him if he were ashamed of his kids.

You'll have to judge for yourself what the right balance is. Take a long look at your friendships with women. How do your kids react to people moving in and out of their lives? You know your kids better than anyone else. If you have considered the possibilities and feel uncomfortable, wait before including your female friends into the times you spend with your kids.

Your kids' ages will have something to do with their reactions. If one of your kids was preschool age at the time of the divorce, he or she was just beginning to develop strong ties with the parent of the opposite sex. Thus, if your preschooler is a girl, she is likely to have some feelings about having caused the divorce through her own developing feelings for you. A parade of women through her life at that time, somewhat connected with you, is bound to create confusion. The same parade of women through a preschool boy's life may cause anxiety because of the ambiguity of his relationships with them and the task which he is attempting to resolve at his stage of development, that of developing his first ties to the opposite sex.

School aged kids can handle the divorce and your women friends more logically. But adolescents may have difficulty adjusting to your female friends. For one thing, the girls may see them as rivals. For another, both adolescent boys and girls may have a hard time understanding that an old person like yourself could be dating. That may not fit the vision they have of their parents.

Say you meet a woman with whom you think you want to share the rest of your life. She and your children have met; they seem to like one another. The kids are not too jealous of the attention you give her. She seems not to begrudge the fact that you have one or more children whom you deeply love and with whom you spend a great deal of time. The kids have seen you hugging and kissing. You, she, and the kids have spent some close times together. Then one day, your kids go into your bedroom, as they often do on the mornings they are with you, and they find you and her together in bed.

Possibly the little ones climb in with you both for a hug before they start the day. Your mate has become part of the ritual. Or perhaps one asks what you are doing, while the others remain silent. You explain to the one who asks, while the other kids are around, that you and Rhonda love each other and want to be together.

You do not belabor the point. If they ask, you tell them. If they do not ask, you do not hold a seminar with charts and graphs. But you do watch for signs as to what they might be thinking and deal with those signs on that level. You watch how they treat Rhonda. Are they acting differently toward her than before? Is any of their behavior different since you made it clear that you are going to share your life with this woman?

For example, your daughter may try to exclude Rhonda from the dinner conversation. See if your daughter will talk about her feelings then. You say, "You have any thoughts about Rhonda and me getting closer?" Maybe there will be some confusion about Rhonda's role. Maybe your daughter is trying to figure out whether Rhonda is like her mother, and is struggling with how she should treat Rhonda. Since she's loyal to her mother, she may not understand that she can respect and learn to love Rhonda without taking away from the respect and devotion that she gives her mother. You can help by clarifying. You explain that your kids have only one mother. Rhonda is not their mother, but you love Rhonda and there is room for that love in the new family you created with your kids.

After working it through with your kids, what happens if the thing with you and Rhonda does not work out? It will probably be sad for you, but what do you tell your kids? That is why we said above that we decided not to run people by them until we were reasonably sure that the relationship would last. They just lived through a

71

separation between you and their mom. They worked through the feelings of abandonment and have been reassured that they were not the cause of the divorce. Now you introduce them to someone else whom you say you love, and who, again, moves out of their lives, perhaps never to be seen again. Maybe they feel that Rhonda couldn't take it because of them. The only thing you can do is to be straight with them. You tell them immediately. And you spend several months working this one through with each of them in their own way, at their own stages. How many times do you want to do that? It can get pretty tiring.

When you are divorced there will be other friendship changes. Not only will there be new women around from time to time, but there will be new male friends as well. Our preteen children were not threatened by old friends who surfaced after the divorce, and they seemed to enjoy the new male friends; they liked the opportunity to be around different adults. However, they were for the most part threatened by the appearance of any new woman.

For example, when meeting a new woman they would ask: "Do you know my mom?" We reasoned this through and decided it was not an attempt to skewer their father. Rather, if they thought the new woman was pretty and smart, they assumed she knew their mother and they wanted to get all of the relationships straight. Also, they compared each woman to their mother. Was she as warm and loving? Would she let them swim after lunch? Did she wear nail polish? Did she work? Any new woman became the surrogate symbol for the missing ingredient of a family.

Given the amount of impact we believe a father's behavior with women will have on his kids, we hesitate to offer prescriptions. But when the kids ask you about being lonely, dating, and how you spend your time when they are not around, you have only two reasonable choices. You can avoid it all with a joke which delays the answer, or you can tell them the truth. But you should not lie to them.


## ECONOMIC ADJUSTMENTS

Sharing your children may cost you a bit more than you expected. At a certain point in your life as a divorced parent, this thought alone can break your spirit. But, like getting in physical shape, you can build up to where you can go a reasonable distance relatively easily. Just be aware that it costs extra money to have a child-sharing plan.

When you have your kids with you for any length of time, there are always extra financial requirements. You will feed them more, for one thing. There are the lost mittens right before you are all ready to go out and play in the snow. You will buy a new pair. If you begin to share the children during any given week, you will have to come up with lunch money, or set up a system where your prepare their lunches. It always seems that when you have everything nailed down—the bags packed, the kids ready to go, teeth cleaned and hair combed, your own day planned with enough cash to get you through until the next time you go to the bank—your kids will remind you that they need lunch money. So you pull out your wallet and give each kid more than the needed amount because you do not have the correct change. Clutching the cash in hand, they look at you with gleaming eyes because they know they are going to finish the day with some extra money. You deliver a lecture (the extra change buys you the right to do it, and ensures that they will at least pretend they are listening). Sounding like Eliot Janeway you caution them against spending the money on junk food. You also plan to eat your lunch for the next several days at the same old sandwich shop where the food to fuel your afternoon tastes like cardboard.

It's a waste of time to try to deduct these incidental expenses from the support payment. It's not worth the time and effort. It will only start a problem of haggling about pennies with your former wife. If you are moving toward a plan of sharing your children with your former wife, you can renogotiate the support payment at a later time and then base it on actual, predictable weekly expenditures.

Even the most obtuse former wife will be unable to avoid knowing that you are contributing financially to your children's daily life above and beyond the support payments. Her understanding of this fact can be beneficial when you are late with the support payment. It is at this moment you can tell her that there is only one economic law: there's no such thing as a free lunch! At the least you'll be building credit and credibility with your ex-wife by assuming some of these additional costs when sharing your children. Just avoid needless haggling, it affects the kids.

Regardless of your financial situation, any additional expenditures will hurt, especially in the early phases of the separation. This is another sacrifice involved in getting in shape for staying active with your children. But, like building up physical stamina, the early part of the program hurts most. Once you've made the new routine a part of your life, the benefits of increased involvement with your children may make you glad you built up your endurance. You begin to economize by fixing your lunch along with theirs.

You have been warned: the children will find ways to ferret out extra money from you. Be prepared to take a stand. However, if you aren't prepared and it sort of creeps up on you one day, try not to feel that you are being used and abused. It is axiomatic: it is going to cost you more to have a child-sharing plan that works.

## PROFESSIONAL CONSIDERATIONS

While talking to divorced dads about their experiences, we found several consistent themes. At the apex was the problem of sharing their kids and earning a living. We have been accused by our divorced dad friends of trying to be both mother and father to our children, and at times—especially during the normal work hours—that does frequently seem to be the case. In order to be actively involved in our preteenaged kids' lives, we make more phone calls during the regular nine-to-five work hours. We spend more time with our kids and probably less time in a number of other areas of our lives. (We mentioned above the abridged social schedule.) We have concluded that while your children are young, you will no doubt have to make some changes in your career.

You know the trite phrase—that a child will lead you. Well, in our cases that is not far from the truth. When our children began to require more time and emotional energy from us, we began to find places where we could get that time. When we looked at how we spent our lives—how anxious we were about our professional lives and how much time and energy being anxious took—we saw where we might get some extra time for our kids.

We are not sure whether our thoughts were propelled by a mid-life crisis, or by the strain of continually being upwardly mobile, but we both decided that our kids were the most important part of our lives and that we could give up some of the anxious hours of our "careers." Time, unlike money and power, is not an expandable part of our lives. Rather, to get more time for one activity we have to take it from another. There is no way to "buy time."

How do you get to spend more time with your kids? Can those extra hours be found? Yes, and if you are honest about how you spend most of your time in your job, you will find that a great deal of it has been spent on nonproductive things. For example, sometimes you stayed late at the office because there was an important project that had to be done with a group of people. They could not get their act together until after five. This meant that you had to stay after quitting time, too. You felt that the project was important, that you had to remain there and work with the group. That was when you were married and knew that your kids were being cared for. Your wife or a babysitter was there, and your kids would understand that you had to work late.

When that began to happen to us as divorced fathers, and there was no one to pick up the kids, we had to face the embarrassment of letting our work partners down. We had to tell them, "I have to get my kids." Some of them looked at us pretty quizzically. Some of them thought we were lying. Some of them secretly admired us because we had said "no" to whoever was in charge. We had told the group that we had something more important to do. We had to get our kids.

The first time it happened we were a little timid. We were concerned about what would happen. However, after we made the stand and left to get our kids (feeling a bit morally superior), we had the feeling that we were no longer owned. Curt Flood must have felt the same way when he said he was not chattel.

We both had careers or jobs which required that we work with other people. Leaving the group in order to handle some problem with one of our kids meant messing up the group's plans. We have learned that it does not happen often, but when it does happen we leave. Important projects have a way of being there and remaining just as important the next day.

You have got to exercise a fair amount of judgment, of course. Tell the kids you will drop whatever you are doing and be with them, but make sure they realize that they cannot call unless they really need you.

It has actually only happened to each of us once. When it did, we went to our kids and the job was done the next day. No one at work was overly concerned. Again, put all this in perspective. We would not expect Henry Kissinger (a divorced dad) while jetting around the Mideast during his tenure as Secretary of State, to drop everything to see his son. But we expect most divorced fathers can get to their kids if there is an emergency.

In order to do so comfortably, you have to get your professional and parental impulses synchronized. We know it is not easy, but from a personal and social point of view, it makes sense to put a career second. You are probably not going to be a full professor at thirty or a vice president at forty. So do not give up your kids because you have unmet career needs.

If more dads spent less time in institutions (corporations, universities, and government) and more time working at home, two things would happen. We assert that productivity would increase, that you would actually do more and better work. Second, your kids would have fewer problems. In the social research-government-university nexus, we have seen dozens of kids and families nearly or actually destroyed because dad was saving the world.

Most of us do not get a chance to do earth-shattering deeds. Even if we did, we could probably have done it better at home. Sound revolutionary? Not really. If you added up your commuting time, coffee breaks, unproductive meetings (the opiate of the upwardly mobile) each day, you would be shocked. Most of the time we have spent in such encounters has only tended to make us fractious and therefore unproductive. The only way to cure this over the long haul is to develop more cottage industries to allow more (especially divorced) dads an opportunity to be at home with their kids. However, until you can get that organized (we are doing more and more work at home), there are some interim suggestions.

First of all, try to make a few moves toward becoming a cottage industry. If you are self-employed, this is fairly easy, and you can get a tax write-off for working regularly at home. If you are institution bound, try to convince your superiors of the wisdom of allowing you to do more work at home. Tell them about wanting to be around your kids more, and that this is one way of doing it. However, they will want to know what advantages they will receive from this experiment. The answer is obvious. Increased productivity is what you give in return.

The next thing you should do is have a talk with your boss. Tell him or her that you may have to leave on a moment's notice if one of your children needs you. You should let your employer know that you are now a divorced parent and that you have responsibilites you did not have before. It isn't necessary to explain all the arrangements, but you can outline the basic plan. Simply put, you are responsible for your children. At times you have to be both mother and father, because that is the way you ensure that you see your kids on a regular basis. What employer would want to make it difficult for you to go to your children when they needed you? Very few.

We are both public policy researchers and work together a good bit of the time as freelance social scientists. As we take each new job—usually for a few months at a time—we make arrangements to ensure that the schools, babysitters, former wives, etc., have our new work numbers and that we can leave at a few minutes' notice.

It does not have to be a big deal. You can avoid the histrionics. You merely have to make a stand that this is what you might have to do. It has been our experience that most employers and clients will indeed facilitate such activities, especially if they can notice positive results. We have seen and supervised a number of divorced dads who have not had regular involvement with their children and who have not had to leave work to be with their kids. We believe that these same dads, for a long time after a divorce or separation, have not been very good at their work. They have been wrapped around the axle trying to figure out what is going to happen to them and their kids. However, in one instance when a divorced dad who worked with us made a larger commitment and asked for some extra time off a few times during what is considered normal work hours, he became a better worker. This experience leads us to a major point.

If you are going to ask the employer or client for an occasional hour or hours during the regular work day, you have to make assurances that whatever work you were doing will be done. There are several choices here. Obviously, as you head out the door, you can take the work and promise to deliver it the next day. Or you can come in early. Either way, assure them that you will complete the job. Most employers are less hidebound than you might think. Most of them would rather see results than view you in the process of not accomplishing anything.

Asking for a little flexibility in advance lets them know that you are serious about your children. Then let them know that you will do the job irrespective of whether you happen to be in your chair at the moment or with your kids while they are barfing their brains out in the school nurse's office. The point here is that if you have made prior arrangements, you probably can do all of the things you must do as a divorced dad with some facility. If you haven't mentioned to your employer that you might have to leave on a moment's notice, and it happens, you might have problems. Plan in advance. Show that you are responsible. Then hope that it rarely, if ever, happens.

Socially, economically, and professionally, you will have to make minor and major adjustments to your life if you regularly share your child. We have tried not to sandbag you in these passages. Along with the adjustments we mentioned, we are sure there are others we suppressed or have yet to encounter. However, when you see the results—when you feel the feedback you get from your kids—the adjustment problems seem to fade. Even concerns about the big ones are replaced by knowing that you are doing something bigger and better than going out on a lot of boring dates or spending late nights at the office. A few weeks of child sharing supplants any concern about the adjustments you have to make in your life.

# 6
## *A Child-Sharing Barometer*

When their mother is not present to act as a buffer, your kids will act differently. It will be a new experience for your children and for you. At times they become almost your peers; at other times they regress to small children who will not want to talk, just hug. The vacillation between these two extremes may cause you some consternation. It should not. Look at these new patterns with excitement. It will be a learning experience for father and children.

The kids *sans* mom will look to their dad for a lot of direction. Your duties will increase. ("Let me see your teeth." Stale sandwiches to extract from lunch boxes.) You will also have to play nurse. Our kids seem to blossom with a fever several times a year just after leaving their mother's house. Along with these different things for a divorced dad to do, there will be all the questions—those usually asked of both parents separately will now be aimed at you alone.

## DREAMS, FEARS, ANXIETIES

Besides the countless questions, there are dreams to talk about. All our children, especially the young ones, had pretty fierce dreams in the early stages of separation and divorce. However, after the child-sharing plan begins to operate with regularity and they know where you live and what your commitment is, the real cinemascopic, panoramic, R-rated thrillers will subside. Here, though, are a few of our kids' dream themes. If you hear similar ones you will understand that at least two or three other kids have had them.

About once a month our youngest kids would dream. We know because they would cry out, first for their mom and then, remembering where they were, for their dad. (Now, upon occasion, they call out for their *dad* at their mom's house.) They were truly extravaganzas, starring a lot of scary people (Darth Vadar and "Jaws") in cameo appearances. Other dreams featured their parents. The kids would dream that they were in a strange neighborhood and couldn't find the way home; that a favorite pet had run away; that someone bad was repossessing the house and they would have to move. After dreams like these, the kids would crawl in bed with their dad, who would assure them "dreams aren't real" and talk to them for a while.

We always assumed that these dreams meant the kids were working things out. We know we dream when we have unsolved problems from the day, and the kids are probably no different. As they have grown used to the divorce and child-sharing arrangements, their abandonment dreams have been less frequent. Most of the kids now dream about struggles with their teachers or worrying about a sick pet. However, all six kids have active fantasies and imaginations and we know there will be more dreams.

Understanding kids' dreams and getting a jump on understanding some of their problems can be done by listening to their questions. That is the first bleep on an early warning screen. The bleep is likely to occur when you are not particularly interested or attuned. Somehow the more important questions get raised by kids during the most unexpected times. While you are shaving one of your kids will enter, nudge you gently, and stand on one foot, then the other. He or she will no doubt sigh heavily a few times and wait for you to say, "What's up, pal?"

"Well, how we gonna work out Christmas?" When this happens in September, your first impulse is to evade the question. But be aware that it may not be Christmas the child is concerned about. He may be thinking about some of the usual Christmas participants (grandfathers, aunts, uncles and cousins, or his mother). He may be concerned about next weekend or his birthday in October. Think and probe a little more about what is really concerning him.

We are not sure if the range of fears and anxieties that kids raise through the question–dream approach is solely related to divorce or a natural function of maturation. Either way we believe it is important to be ready to help them first differentiate between dreams and real life, and then help resolve the real concern.

Answering questions and dealing with dreams are both parts of the same divorced dad activity—keeping the lines of communication open. One of our children, for example, often asks, "How long will Tubby live?" Your kid will probably ask the same type of question when you have just burned the spaghetti sauce and are really thinking about how to afford new snow tires. Your first impulse is to say, "How the hell should I know?" Be cool. You can cook more sauce and charge the tires at Sears. What you may not be able to do is keep the lines of communication open if you snap at them when they question you about the family. A better response is, "Tubby is a little overweight, but he is a pretty healthy dog and should live for ten or fifteen years. Why are you worried about him?" This kind of answer will let them know you believe their questions are important and that you want to explore them further. It will not close out discussion. If there is anything beyond a concern about how long they can expect their pet to be with them, this gives you the opportunity to find out and to talk about it.

Answering questions has two functions. The first and most obvious one is that they will get a substantive reply ("your dog is healthy"); the second is symbolic. They will have proof that you care and are concerned about the issues they raise. Yes, you are divorced from their mother. No, you will not leave them.

Sometimes when they ask questions, you will discover that they have opened some new doors for you. For example, a couple of our kids (the older ones, both girls) have shown an inordinate amount of concern about what we do when they are not around. They ask, "Where were you last night? I called you at 8:00, 8:30 and 9:00."

This kind of question means one of your kids is concerned about what you do when you are not with them. When one or more of them asks you this question, you may be put off at first. You may think your former wife is prying—getting one of your kids to do her intelligence gathering. Probably your kid is just concerned about your life when he's not with you. How should you handle this? We believe that unless you were out clandestinely planning to rob a bank or mount a secret invasion of

84

Mexico, you should tell them what you were doing. After a few times, they will give up. They will not be as interested in your every moment.

A story about another divorced dad and his child is relevant here. An eight-year-old friend of one of the Shepard daughters asked what "Mr. Shepard" thought about her dad. She said she called to tell her dad (who was divorced and lived about 200 miles from her home in Boston) that he hadn't kept his promise to come to see her on her birthday. "But," she said, "he was not at home even late, about 12:00 at night. Where do you divorced dads go at night?" A little later in the conversation, she wanted to know (given that she had a divorced dad as a captive audience) what she should do to get her dad to come to see her.

She was told to write her dad a letter. Sad advice. And how many other kids are there who call their dad at night, or wonder when or if he will ever visit them? Divorced dads should think long and hard before they break promises.

If the surface had been scratched when that eight-year-old asked about her dad, a lot of things would have been uncovered. You could start with the layer which was concern about the birthday, and then meet successive layers, like onion peels. You would have uncovered more and more until you got to the nub—her desire to see her dad. It was not, we discovered in other conversations, the missed birthday; it was the missed dad. This particular vignette reminds us of another conversation with our kids and their peers—another conversation about divorce.

The Goldman kids threw their skis and poles into the back of the car and climbed in. They had just ended their Friday afternoon lesson, sponsored jointly by their school and a local ski area. They talked about the kids in their class and others they met on the hill. Kathryn began to describe a boy she had not seen before, but met riding the lift. "His parents are divorced, too," she said.

That was a real eye-opener. Kathryn is a fine conversationalist, but she does not start up new conversations easily. The lift ride is no more than five minutes. What was going on in her mind which would prompt her to talk about her parents' divorce to a stranger in so short a time? She rarely talks directly about the divorce. She seems to understand the arrangement which her parents made and has not expressed much fear or anxiety about it. Yet, if that is how she introduces herself to a new person, the divorce must loom larger than she indicates outwardly.

This time, instead of a question, it was careful listening which cast new light on a child's perception of divorce. Throughout their pre-majority years, we believe you will have to listen for signals that they want you to talk to them. That is what married dads do, or should do, and divorced dads may have to be even more sensitive to keep communication open and flowing freely.

Of course, divorce is a difficult time for all the family, and it is a particularly difficult time for kids. They may have some thoughts about the role they played in the separation and divorce. They may feel that if it were not for their presence, you and your former wife would be married still. They might ask you if taking care of them is an ordeal. Or they might suggest that, but for them, you could be doing something else at the moment, or with your whole life, which would be more fulfilling for you.

Although interpreting their questions and dreams is subjective at best, you can track what they continue to say or dream and look at the themes. These things are clues to what their concerns are, or to what they are working through in their minds.

As we have discovered, thoughts of the divorce and

the family's cleavage are ever-present in the consciousness of even the coolest kid. Although children may appear to handle things well, listen hard to what they are saying and asking. Listening helps you know how the child sharing is going and how the kids are adjusting to the family's split.

## DEFUSING EMOTIONAL PROBLEMS

You cannot minimize the divorce. It will affect your kids' outlook and the way they live their lives. *Any* major—or minor— childhood experience will shape their lives. However, divorce need not block your children's development.

We say and we believe that divorce need not destroy your kids' lives, but we need to give you a little more information to make you feel comfortable with this thought. There may be some instances in which one or more of your children will need to talk to or be evaluated by a counselor. It happened that both the Shepard and Goldman families had a couple of sessions with a counselor about a specific child problem during the early part of their separations. Each of us still has mixed feelings about the episode. But there may be times when just loving, sharing, and paying attention to your kid is not enough.

We cannot foresee when those times may arise. Rather, we want to describe our feelings and thoughts about how it happened with our kids—when one or both parents thought it was time to seek help from someone other than a friend or relative. One of us has been a psychiatric social worker who worked with kids, and the other has completed several studies related to kids. Even though we have been studying and working with young people for a long time, both families talked to a coun-

selor. We have been this route and think it was illumi-
nating. So it may take more than loving or caring. You
may feel you need outside help, as we both did.

If you are paying attention to your kids, you can sense
their moods. You will know when something is bothering
them and when they are contented. You will learn how
to get each one to talk about his or her problems. You
will know that each child needs to be handled a bit
differently. As an active father you had experience dealing with each of their particular crises. As you build a
solid base and routine with your kids after the divorce,
you find that they talk more freely with you about their
lives. And they seek your advice and help more easily.
For the most part you and your kids feel able to deal
with the crises in all your lives and to keep the helping
one another within the family circle.

But, if the circumstances surrounding the divorce or
any other major experience in your kids' lives are so
overwhelming that they need more than common sense
and love, how do you tell when they need professional
help?

First, remember their ages at the time the separation
occurred. Since many child-development professionals
believe that the earliest years are the most impressionable
and set the course of one's life, the older the child at the
time of separation, the more equipped he or she will be
to deal with it successfully. This applies only generally.
The circumstances surrounding the separation will have
a lot to do with any child's life adjustment, regardless
of his or her age when it happened.

As a general rule the younger ones will be more confused, more vulnerable to the events, and more seriously
affected. This is especially so if they have developed a
recognition of and a relationship with both parents.
Therefore, we're talking about any child between the
ages of two to approximately six or seven. The chances

are that they will have more difficulty handling the separation than their younger or older siblings. The older ones will be able to deal with it more rationally. The younger ones will not have as firmly developed relationships, particularly with their father.

## WHEN PROFESSIONAL HELP IS NEEDED

Many problems can be worked out with love, understanding, patience, and time, by focusing your attention and presence on the problem at hand. "Staying with" your child when he is troubled may be half the battle. Those are not earthshaking statements. But the step to professional counseling is a big one and the discipline is not a panacea for all emotional problems. We refer to therapists here as all *certified* professionals providing assistance with emotional problems, including psychiatrists, psychologists, lay therapists and social workers.

Your kids may have difficulty describing what they feel to you, a person with whom they feel comfortable. When you take them to a shrink, they're introduced into an alien environment and expected to develop a rapport with a complete stranger. True, there are various techniques which put children at their ease. For the very young, play therapy enables them to act out their feelings through playing with toys or dolls in the presence of a skilled therapist. But for the most part the child is expected, sooner or later, to tell the doctor where it hurts.

Unless a child is seriously disturbed, the relationship with the shrink takes on parts of the relationship which the child has—or should have—with his or her parents. The counselor is a trusted friend with whom the child can discuss problems and in whom the child can confide. The shrink takes the place of that part of the parent which the parent cannot provide, for whatever reason. But, if you've been staying actively involved with your kids, you'll have developed the necessary trusting type of relationship with them. To be sure, there are sides of family life which may never be satisfactory for parents and children, whether the parents are married or divorced. Certain parent/child relationships, or certain parts of them, may set both parties on edge and erode the potential love and trust between parent and child. A father, no matter how hard he tries, may be cold and domineering. A child, for no apparent reason, may be recalcitrant and difficult. But even in circumstances such as these, a shrink is not the automatic answer. Before contacting him, be sure that you have said to yourself: "I've exercised all the patience and understanding that I can muster; the problem has not improved even a small bit."

Most of the problems we've encountered with our kids have been resolved eventually, through our active participation in helping the kids solve them. Problems usually begin with the child having difficulty over a specific issue. The child has recurrent fears and dwells on them, and a pattern is established which the child repeats over and over again. You and the child communicate at some level about it. You try to make any *realistic* adjustments in his or her routine or in your behavior which you believe will bring about some sort of solution. The word *realistic* is important. One of the ways that you will know if your kid needs outside help is if his needs, expectations, or behavior move outside your family's reality. For example, if he exhibits destructive behavior on his way to and from school to the extent that homeowners or police repeatedly complain, the answer is not to establish a regular pattern of taking time off from work to drive him to and from school. You may want to do this as a beginning step, but with the understanding that you will not continue to do it forever. The *reality* is that you have your commitments, as he has his. Realistically, both of you must keep them. You can ease off a little to help him, but he is expected to function in the world like everyone else. If you attempt to take him to and from school to avoid trouble, you are likely to find out that he will exhibit the same behavior elsewhere. And then where are you? Spending all your days driving around with your kid so he will not get into trouble?

In this instance a program of going with him and picking him up in a gradually decreasing sequence might be helpful. The decrease may be worked out between you and your kid, depending on what he feels he needs. The important point is that you and he are participating together in resolving his problem. If you lick it together, you'll have a basis for resolving other problems, either present or future.

But suppose this same destructive behavior persists, either on the way to or from school or at other times. You have used up all the reality-based methods for helping your boy overcome the problem. So the next step is a shrink.

As in all other disciplines, there are good and bad therapists. Some have saved people's lives. Others have just taken their money. Sometimes a shrink can save one patient's life and only take another's money. Aside from the relative merits of individual talents and developed skills (we believe that the discipline is more art than science still), finding the right one is several parts luck and a major portion of chemistry.

Given America's adulation of all fields of medicine, most of us find it difficult to shop for services. We tend to take the first name in the *Yellow Pages* or the first referral from a friend or another doctor. This is absolutely the wrong way to find help.

You can begin an inquiry by contacting your local major hospital or community mental health center. Ask about the range of services they offer and determine if any therapist has divorce or children of divorce as a specialty. Make an appointment. Don't take your child, but do take your former wife. The first rule of selection is: The person from whom you are seeking help must be warm and friendly to you. You must like, and believe you will trust, him or her. If you don't get immediate (in a half hour or so) good vibrations, end the interview and keep searching. You should not be timid about saying you do not like a particular therapist. If you don't feel positive about that person at first, chances are you won't as time goes on, either. Rule number two is: Both you and your former wife will have to participate if your kid is to be helped; therefore, both of you will have to agree upon the therapist. If you follow these basic rules and are willing to shop around, you will find someone who can help. Finally, don't be afraid to ask how much the initial sessions will cost. This is important. The shrink will evaluate your child as the first step, and you should know how much it is going to cost and what will happen during the sessions.

Do not think that just because you've found a counselor and sent your youngster there you've solved the problem. At that point you have only taken an initial step. Your involvement in the process, and also your former wife's involvement, are extremely important. The child didn't create his problems out of thin air. His parents' relationship with each other and their relationship with him may be part of the difficulties he is experiencing. So his problem is not an isolated one but is one which involves the entire family. It is more realistic at that point to give up some time and expend your efforts with the shrink than it is to be at your kid's side constantly through the day to keep him out of trouble.

There have been a number of times when we have been on the verge of going into therapy with our kids.

In two instances we actually started, then turned back. Both times the negative chemistry between ourselves and the shrinks caused us not to continue on that path. And we both admit that the negative chemistry was as much our fault as theirs. Here is what happened.

One of the Goldman children began the first grade of a new school just after her parents separated. Her mom and dad were extra supportive about walking her to school, picking her up at the end of the day, and talking with her teacher. Her sister also went to the same school, and eventually both girls settled in and made the adjustment. She was fearful at first, and several times stayed home when she was not ill; but after the Thanksgiving break, she seemed to accept the routine.

She is a bright, sociable little girl and very interested in the other children in her class. She has no trouble with the actual school work. So she felt plenty of ambivalence. If she did not go to school she would miss everything that was going on with her friends as well as learning some new things. On the other hand, she really liked hanging around with either her mom or her dad all to herself, to play games and be fed and generally taken care of.

The second year she repeated the same pattern. Only this time she began to dwell on the school work expectations which the teacher had for the children. She would carry these thoughts home and have bad dreams about them. One Saturday night when she was with her dad, she woke him up to tell him that she couldn't sleep because she was thinking about the homework which was due the following Monday. She couldn't help it; she just kept thinking about it. Both her dad and mom met with the teacher at various times throughout the fall to clarify what the teacher's expectations were. In all instances they were not as stringent as the child described, to her parents or to herself.

Her mother and father began to talk about a shrink. Both agreed that the whole family would go if necessary. At the same time both parents began to consider ways of making her feel more secure in her life surrounding school. Her mother made an extra effort to be home when she got there each afternoon. (Her mother's job was making her late about half the time during the week.) Her dad spent extra time with her listening to her talk about school. Whenever there was a real problem raised (in her mind), her dad let her know that he would go to school a bit early the next morning and talk it over with her teacher. He did this once, and she never asked him to do it again. Just knowing that he would go seemed to satisfy her.

In the meantime her mom made an appointment to see the school psychologist, and an appointment for the whole family to see a private child guidance and family counselor. The meeting with the school psychologist was unsatisfactory. The psychologist went over the child's aptitude scores and did not seem to connect with the problem being brought to her attention. It was as if the family were bleeding, and the shrink were trying to dispense an aspirin instead of applying a bandage or tourniquet.

Fortunately the child seemed to turn around and relinquish her fears without outside assistance, and by the time the appointment with the private shrink was imminent, her behavior was so much less troubled that both parents cancelled the appointment with a great deal of relief.

Several things happened here. First, the parents responded to their child's need in realistic ways: not with confusion and anxiety, but with active steps taken in collaboration with their child to assure her that they loved her. They assured her that they were available to go to the teacher with her; that they were at home when she got there; and that they were willing to listen calmly to what was bothering her if she could ever express it. Much of the support was non-verbal: being there; going to the teacher; backing her up: "If you ever need me, I'll be there and I'll *help* you when you need me; I won't make it worse by scolding or taking it as a personal reflection on me, or allowing the teacher to make me and you look like a couple of cream puffs."

Second, the school psychologist didn't connect with her mom. Who knows what went on between them? But a need was not met. A human being seeking help with emotional problems was somehow turned away. It happens all the time. That's why we said above that the nature of the relationship with the shrink is many parts chemistry and several parts skill and talent. Too bad for the school shrink. Had a connection been made, the child's parents would have continued seeing her, or the private doctor, until the problem got better. And they would have insisted to anyone who would listen that going to a therapist was the best possible choice. They would have given the shrink all the credit, never discovering in themselves some of what it takes to keep kids on a straight track.

The episode with the youngest Shepard child was a little different. He was acting out a great deal in his mother's presence and would have fierce outbursts at school. The content and context were different, but he was a bit of a problem. Any disagreements with his dad were usually silent confrontations ending with, "I'm not going to tell you—you can't make me!"

Both parents talked to his teachers and discovered that at school he would become very angry about some small incident. His anger manifested itself by outright refusal to participate in group events, and once he kicked a wastebasket. You may, at this point, believe that he was behaving like a lot of other young first and second grade boys. That may be true, but given the separation and divorce, his mother was concerned that the stone in his shoe would become an emotional boulder. His father was not as convinced, but went along with having his son see a psychiatrist. The mother made arrangements and informed the father that they were to talk at least twice to the shrink, and this was done. After several weeks, the psychiatrist asked to have both Shepards available to hear his assessment. From the father's point of view, it went badly.

First of all, it is hard to believe that someone could care about the physical and mental well-being of a child if he placed the kid to be treated in a small, albeit fancy, room and blew smoke in his face. He came to the meeting with the best psychiatric credentials and a Viennese accent. He looked credible, sounded like at least a nephew of Anna Freud, and had all the environmental trappings—bright pictures on the walls and chairs close to the floor. However, Dr. X could hardly be seen through the blue smoke which encased him on his perch.

He began by telling the Shepards that he felt their son had some "unresolved issues" about the divorce, that the son was "stuck" and he should be helped out of that particular pattern. He showed the parents drawings supposedly done by their child—a father fox who left his pups in a dark hole, and a fisherman who was doomed never to catch a fish. Two pictures were sufficient, in Dr. X's mind, to warrant his seeing their son twice a week for a year or so.

However, one of the two pictures flashed quickly before the parents' eyes—that of the fox and pups— was not their son's artwork. The parents expressed consternation at this mistake. The father then went on to ask, "What will you do during those sessions? What is the therapy like? How will you un-stick him?"

Dr. X found these questions "threatening" and replied, "I am going to help him resolve the divorce. I'm going to tell him all about it!"

This dismayed the father. "How are you going to tell my son about our divorce when I have not discussed it with you?" he retorted.

Dr. X then quickly replied that he "had other kids to help" and did not need our business. On this hostile note, Dr. X left the Shepard child's life. Both parents, after a few heated conversations, agreed to think about it and watch their son closely, rather than have any more battles about the efficacy of Dr. X's mystic treatment plan.

The lessons learned from this experience were personally and economically costly ($900 for the evaluation). We now knew that one parent could not just go off and get a shrink without the other's involvement. If both parents are not involved from the first day of searching, it will probably only result in yet another battle.

Just the thought of trying to find a good shrink may convince you that you can handle the child's problem yourself. Pay more attention to your kid's outbursts or to behavior you don't think is healthy. Talk with your former wife about how the child is acting (but see the following section). Talk to other people you know who are involved with children in a professional way before taking the leap. It's no disgrace to see a shrink, but that leap, like many other ventures into the mental health world, can just as easily come a cropper as turn out a helpful experience. Paraphrasing a slogan of the 60s: "When you need a shrink, you can't find one."

## MOTHERS AND FATHERS TOGETHER

"Adult chauvinism!" cried the oldest Shepard child when her mother told her that she and her dad had talked about her when she was not present. "You didn't discuss that with me before you told my dad!" she forcefully informed her mother. We now believe she was right; if the particular problem you are talking about is serious, the accused should have the right in a divorce/child-sharing arrangement to confront her accusers. We believe you must act quite differently from when you were married when it comes to talking about your kids.

When you were married you no doubt talked about problems when the kids were not around. Probably this took place after getting into bed, when you thought about your family, finances, sex, or all three. It seemed all right to talk about your kids when they were not around. But the game changes in divorce.

First of all, if you talk about one or all of your kids when they are not around and they find out about it—which they are more likely to do in a child-sharing arrangement—they will wonder why their parents are talking about them. Then they are probably going to become upset at not knowing what is going on. There is no natural way in which they can find out—the evening meal, for example, or an isolated chat with both parents on Saturday morning or Sunday afternoon when the rest of the world's problems subside. Next, if you are serious about actually solving the problem, they have to be part of the solution. Be straight and honest about their alleged fears or behavior.

The other reason one has to include the child in the discussion is that under a child-sharing arrangement, you don't want one of the parents to become the problem identifier and the other the solver. Discipline and solving minor problems should be done with all three people present. In this way you will not be accused of being an "ageist" or adult chauvinist. It will also let the kid know that both parents are involved and equally responsible for sanctions.

Along these lines, if both parents and kids are involved when there is a problem to discuss, there is less possibility that either the parent or the kid can manipulate the other. This is important because divorce and child sharing can indeed be golden opportunities to polish or develop nascent political and manipulation skills. Don't let it happen.

These are a few of the important things we learned about our kids from our direct experience with them in child sharing after divorce. After a lot of fits and starts, things are going well. Now we're planning for the future, when our children will be teenagers.

## LIVES OF THEIR OWN

None of our offspring are adolescents yet. Our oldest are perched on the cusp. While their parents are still the primary people in their lives, they are beginning to make the transition to independent personhood. They're not as malleable as they once were. When we make decisions for the whole family, we have to explain why to them. And if the explanation is not good enough, they may not go along with the plan: "I don't want to visit my grandmother. I don't care if she likes to see me. I love her, but it's boring." A harbinger of growing up and breaking away from the family.

According to the experts, adolescence is when all the unresolved problems of childhood hit the fan for one last dramatic go-round. After that they go underground and emerge, like the groundhog looking for his shadow, at various mid-life stages. One reason that adolescence is so turbulent is that the tasks at this stage of personal development—gaining independence and identity, achieving occupational or educational goals, becoming a sexual being—all collide with the unresolved problems.

An ever-present question lurks at the edges of parents' minds. What is going to happen to our kids in adolescence? It's there, in part, because every parent is aware that his kids' upbringing was imperfect. The results of those imperfections are likely to show up in adolescence and to be as devastating as a flash summer storm washing out a roadbed.

For us the questions are: How will the divorce affect them? Was the child-sharing plan a good way to ward off some of the turbulence? Did it help resolve some of the problems which the divorce introduced? We don't know yet. But we envision some changes in the kids' lives and our own.

In the child-sharing years we are quite close to our children during the time we spend with them. We are not with them always, so we interact a great deal when we are together. That means a lot of shared activities and time spent talking with one another. Because our kids are not always around, we don't take the time with them for granted. And dad and kids seem to make an extra effort to pay attention to one another. By saying this we are not putting down a "normal" family life where mother and father are constantly there. Taking for granted also implies a sense of security about that person. Our kids may have less of that. But you pays your money and you takes your choice.

As fathers caught up in the economic struggle for survival, our times with our kids are a welcome and relaxed change from battling the world, playing adult status games, or trying to figure out what some other supposedly grownup individual or group is trying to say to us through their ambivalent behavior. If the truth be known, we value our times with our kids as islands of sanity in a pretty crazy world. Kids are simple, truthful, and playful. The rest of the world rarely is. So it's nice to be around them and we look forward to those times.

When the kids get into adolescence, their main task will be to break away from us. They will need to move from our influence to establish their own identities. Their peer groups may be more important than their family groups. They will be more interested in what is going on outside the home—in that powerful and compelling teenage culture, whatever it will be for them.

These days we can pile the kids in the car and go anywhere, and it will be a big adventure. When they are adolescent they won't pile into the car as readily, not only because their larger sizes won't be conducive to piling, but because they may want to go in separate directions. Mealtimes are currently a collaborative venture: everyone plays some part in getting us all to the table together with warm food before us. It's a time for the kids to talk seriously about what bothers them, or playfully about anything in the world. But mealtime may become more random. For a while, or maybe for the rest of their lives, they won't think it's neat to sit and talk with dad. It may be more important to talk with a best friend peer.

These days our kids think it is a big treat to spend some time with either parent. But in adolescence they will not. No doubt they will view us as a bit old-fashioned, since they will be trying to break away from us, from the nest, from our values. They may feel funny being with us at times, especially as they go through a stage of rejecting our values to establish their own.

What can you do about all this? You let them go. As Gibran says in *The Prophet:* "You are the bows from which your children as living arrows are sent forth. . . . For their souls dwell in the house of tomorrow, which you cannot visit, not even in your dreams." And the best way that you can let them go is to prepare for it when your kids are preadolescent.

We say this because we've set out a plan for you to

be actively involved with your kids. But it's not a static course. There are changes at each age level, and the most dramatic one will be at adolescence.

During your children's early years, you will be building a pattern of closeness. They will depend on you for a major part of their personal life education. But at some point you will change from the font of knowledge, power, entertainment, and sustenance to a backdrop in their lives. If you have invested a lot of emotional energy in being with your kids, the change may be hard on you both. If your kids are a focal point in your life, you may not be prepared for their not wanting to be with you as much, not taking you as seriously as they did only a year or a few months ago.

The best thing you can do for your children at that stage is to let them go, but let them know that you'll be there when they need you. The best thing you can do for yourself, if you have been actively involved with your kids, is to create a parallel independent life while they are still close to you. That life should consist of interests, friends, and ways to entertain yourself when your kids are not around. We sound like counselors for the middle-aged wife whose children are grown and whose husband is all wrapped up in his work. Well, the same advice holds for you and for us.

It is not as if you will never see your kids once they reach adolescence. The pattern in our society seems to be that the kids move back and forth from the nest for a relatively long time. Some will come home to touch base periodically. Others may want to live with you for prolonged spans. The way our society and economic structure are currently established, adolescence is a prolonged stage which often does not end with the teens, but may extend well into the twenties and possibly beyond. In fact, there has been a trend in the 1970's for children in their twenties to return home to live with their parents indefinitely. Economic pressure may cause them to stay with you longer than they would have when there were more jobs available.

After your kids reach adolescence the relationship which you have built with them is sure to change. But it need not evaporate. On the contrary, if you have created a solid personal life of your own you will enjoy years of the changing patterns of your kids' development. It will be different from when you were working out the child-sharing plan. But if you don't live your whole life through or for your kids, and if you let them go when they are ready, you will find your subsequent time with them fulfilling in other ways. Who knows—maybe someday they'll pile you into the car and take you to a movie.

## KIDS AND NEW WIVES

One of us has remarried, and part of the success of that remarriage has and will no doubt continue to hinge upon how the new wife and the kids relate. Being the wife of a divorced dad—whether or not she has been married or has kids of her own—is a difficult role. It cannot be that of a surrogate mother. It is not that of someone the father is dating. And, initially, it is not an equal partner in raising the kids even on a part-time basis. These are a few of the things that a new wife of a divorced father cannot be, though the reasons may not be obvious.

If the divorced dad has preteen daughters there is a very good chance they are crazy about him. In fact, when the mother and father were divorced the daughter may have secretly and fleetingly thought that this was an opportunity for her, the daughter, to be in the cat bird seat with her dad. If you have a preteen daughter and are a married or divorced dad, you will know what we are talking about here. Having preteen daughters is great; they adore you and will usually listen to your advice. But hold your hat when a new woman, or even their mother, seems to be a threat. If the interloper is the mother, it can be worked out. If, on the other hand, the woman between you and your preteen daughter is someone you are dating or have recently married, the result may be a familial donnybrook. To avoid trouble between the new woman in the divorced dad's life and his preteen daughters, here are some simple and workable ideas.

If you are about to remarry, or if you are dating or cohabiting, you should talk over the situation separately with your mate and children. Tell the kids, "You may have guessed that Rhonda is moving in." Wait for their response. If they feel strongly that Rhonda is not a potential candidate for sainthood or the Nobel peace prize, and are bold enough to tell you so, do not let it throw you. They probably will not be ecstatic about *anyone* moving in, and you will have to view what they say in light of that. Also, if you and your kids are in the middle of rebuilding your relationship, they may be really upset by the possibility of someone moving in. They are bound to compare the new woman to their mother. Their conclusions may not be impartial.

The other side of the human equation also has to be apprised of how the kids feel about her. If she has not been around children before, then the introduction has to be in small doses. You will have to give her time to get used to kids and to what it is like in your "family." She will have to be aware of what it will take to define her role with the kids.

The most crucial thing is to give everyone involved enough time to make adjustments.

Some of the questions the kids will ask are: "Do we have to do what she says? What will she do here? Does she like plain or pepperoni pizza? Can we still watch TV in your bed with you? Will she make us clean up our rooms? Will she always ride in the front seat with you? How old is she? Does she have any kids?" These are some of the potpourri of questions you can expect.

On the new mate's side, she will have a few questions herself that need to be answered. "What'll I do when they say no? Are they always that loud in the morning? Can I ask them not to chew with their mouths open? What do you like to eat? Do you think they like me?" She will no doubt be nervous, and you as a divorced dad will have to remember that she is entering not just your life but your family, a group in which its members already know where they stand with each other and how hard they can push on certain issues. It is a very difficult role for any new mate and you will at times find that you are a mediator in a silent war, with sides drawn but issues not clearly defined. In most of these instances you will have to first clarify the issues which seem to be emerging between your new mate and the kids. Then you will have to solve these ill-defined problems.

You may think you have a difficult life role, but you must remember that the new mate's and the kids' positions are equally, if not more, difficult. And they do not have the power you do. So when you feel the tensions building, when one of your kids spills his milk at dinner and announces that the brown rice casserole is not like his mother's, be aware that it is natural and in time these issues will subside . . . only to be replaced by more serious ones.

Among these more serious issues to emerge after the initial rounds of hostility have evaporated is one of who's in charge when you are not around. Kids will probably not leap with joy at yet another adult entering their lives to give them advice. But however unpleasant for the kids, you have to make a stand and let them know that you trust Rhonda and her judgment, and when you are not around she is in charge.

At the same time you will have to temper Rhonda's power and authority impulses: urge her to govern wisely and as little as possible. Hopefully Rhonda is older than your oldest child and loves you enough to understand how difficult, yet rewarding, her new position will be. Her position is somewhat analogous to many of our recent vice presidents; they were selected for other than governing skills, yet many of them had to assume the role quickly and under difficult circumstances. Tell Rhonda how difficult it was for Ford and Lyndon Johnson when they were second in command and then had to lead a cabinet they did not select. It can be done, but it isn't easy.

You will have to be the early warning system for bad vibrations between Rhonda and the kids. There will be a fair number of touchy times, but get at them early and try to remember that your kids *are* kids, and that Rhonda—no matter how much of a neophyte at ruling she is—is an adult. You will have to consider her thoughts and emotions, not to the detriment of your children, but as the first among those you love. You have got to keep a lot of balls in the air, but always remember how difficult things must be for Rhonda and the kids.

You should be sensitive to Rhonda's feelings about what may seem to be insignificant events. Ask her before planning family events. Ask her about when she would like dinner (kids are always ready). Ask her which movie she would like to see. These may seem unimportant, but they are not. She will appreciate having her views considered, especially when the children are to be included. Asking her opinion in matters such as these is probably the most important thing you can do.

Next, be willing to tell her not to get caught in the

crossfire between you and your kids, or between two of your kids. Tell her to avoid most of these instances until she feels comfortable with jumping in and providing a solution and following through. She must understand that it may take several months or even years to gain legitimacy in your kids' eyes as a problem-solver and giver of sanctions. However, if you have laid the foundation and Rhonda has not been too quick in trying to gain the legitimacy, it will work.

Another area for caution is that of having Rhonda becoming a confidante or friend of the kids, taking their side in opposition to their mother or you. This is one of the easier roles for Rhonda to assume. But it will not work.

You will have to set the tone for the relationship. Discuss with both Rhonda and the kids how difficult her position is. Tell them and her that she will not replace their mother. Tell both camps that she is another adult in their lives who will—you are sure—grow to love them, and they her. But it will indeed take time. Tell both camps not to let little things grow out of proportion, to let each other know what is bugging them before it becomes serious enough for you to intervene. This last point is of major importance.

If a disagreement or battle reaches the boiling point and the divorced dad has to intervene, probably everyone will lose. You will have to make a decision which, if you act in the tradition of Solomon, will be wise and just and probably unpopular with both camps. So tell *them* to work it out. Next there is a problem of how and when Rhonda will direct the kids whether or not you are around. Do not let her rely on your legitimacy and natural authority. For example, if one of the kids is doing something that annoys Rhonda, and all three of you are present, and she says, "Ask Suzy to stop slurping her granola!"—do not respond. Rhonda will have to understand she must build her own reservoir of authority and ask Suzy directly to stop that annoying behavior. Suzy, on the other hand, will have to understand that her behavior would indeed annoy any adult at 7:30 A.M. and that Rhonda is not being bitchy.

Nothing very complicated here. You just have to remember not to let problems become serious. Give Rhonda and the kids time to get their relationship straight. When you take sides, be sure you have thought about the short and long-term implications of your acts.

Balancing just a wife and several kids is surely enough emotional involvement for a man if it is done right. When the wife becomes your former wife, and Rhonda enters—and Rhonda is not sure about the old relationship (is it ever over?) you have enough emotional content for several lives, let alone yours. However difficult it may be to think about this rectangle, it has to be part of your thinking and behavior.

There is no real way to convince a present spouse that the former wife is out of the picture, especially when she is not out of the picture because you are sharing the kids with her. So we can scratch that argument.

How is your ex-wife in the picture? Well, you have to talk to her about the economics of your relationship. This will take some time even if everything is worked out. Even when a divorced dad is doing fine financially, the cash flow as opposed to income may become a problem. If you have to be a few days late with the first wife's check, you had better tell her. It will lower her anxiety; she will not have the chance to say that the kids' father has not paid, and therefore Suzy cannot have new shoes and they cannot afford pizza on Friday night.

The first wife is in the picture when a kid is sick and you cannot transport him on the regular schedule, and you each call several times to find out how he is doing. The new wife answers several phone calls per week from the former wife, and all of a sudden it gets to her. There is no real answer. Just keep saying that it is necessary for two people living apart and sharing their children to talk to each other. Sorry for the inconvenience, Rhonda, but that's the way it is.

We called this chapter "A Child-Sharing Barometer" because we've learned the importance of detecting storms early on. You can do something about the family, unlike the weather, but it helps to know as soon as possible that trouble is brewing. If you are sensitive to your kids' questions and dreams; if you don't simply hope that major problems will disappear; if you don't go behind your kids' backs; if you get ready for their adolescence; and if you prepare the kids for your new wife (and vice versa)—you'll be pretty busy. But you'll be a lot happier.

# 7
## Our Kids Have Their Say

As we were thinking about writing a book on being a divorced dad, we had several conversations with our kids. They were excited about seeing their names in print and possibly going to their local library and finding— amidst the encyclopedias and yellowed newspapers—a book about them. We then told them that some of the time spent writing "the book" would mean less time with them and that some of the meals they like would disappear during this time, to be replaced by easier-to-prepare ones. They seemed willing to give a little. Hopefully, the experience of listening to their dads discuss and argue about what was to be said in each chapter, as well as the actual time spent writing, was not a big encroachment on their time with us. However, what probably made the most sense to them was that, if there was going to be a book, they would get an opportunity to have their say. And they did.

It was a dreary Saturday morning. The Goldman and Shepard kids were ready. They had been told for several days that it was going to happen on Saturday. They had been filled with special pancakes and real Vermont maple syrup. The fire was blazing in the fireplace, and as we all sat looking at the rain and mud outside, the air inside was filled with creative tension. Who was going to go first?

## ADJUSTING TO THE DIVORCE

"Why d'ya wanna know about divorce? I'm not even married yet!" was the first response from a young Goldman daughter—a funny second grader. From that we went on to a series of questions about what they liked and disliked about the divorce and subsequent child-sharing arrangements. We told them they were the experts and we wanted to know how they thought their living arrangements were working out.

They were initially melodramatic as they remembered back to the days in which their parents were deciding to split. "I thought my life was going down the tubes. I cried every night to myself," said one of the daughters, a usually noncommittal and easygoing ten-year-old. Once that had been said by one of the kids, they all sort of nodded, and then did not feel the need for more drama and remembering how sad they were. Another added, "We don't have to listen to the fighting and yelling anymore, and besides, we get more attention from our parents now."

Some of the above remarks may seem predictable to divorced parents, and they may therefore wonder why we bothered. The obvious answer is that you never know until you ask and listen to what is said. We know, for example, that no one had any fun during the initial stages

111

of separation and divorce. We did not need to ask our kids about that. However, what we could not have really predicted was the extent to which the kids (all of them) saw the child-sharing arrangement as a positive and important part of their lives. Or at least we did not predict what parts they say are the most important and what parts are troublesome.

They each reported in a different way that they did not know in advance that their parents would help them work out a new life, one in which they would not have to listen to the "fighting and yelling" anymore. What they saw, initially, was one sad shaky parent taking care of them, and one parent who wasn't around much in the first days of the separation; all this on the heels of a lot of "fighting and yelling." Once a new structure, a child-sharing plan, became a visible part of their lives, the children began to put their internal lives in order around it.

So a new adjustment takes time, and it takes the effort of both parents creating a consistent plan. That may not be too surprising. But if there were no consistent effort by the parents to actually *accompany* their kids through the divorce experience, we believe that our children would not talk about a "before" and an "after" so easily. They might not be able to make the distinctions between now and then with such clarity.

## HAVING TWO HOMES

Our kids talked of the many new parts of their lives which they had to get used to at the time of the separation. Always being away from one parent was the first and hardest part of the new arrangement. They missed the absent parent. Having a split week under an equal child-sharing plan was the best antidote to this. Our kids felt that the split week enabled them to keep from missing the absent parent if they knew they would see him or her soon. A week away from either parent seemed too long a time.

In both our cases the dads had to create a new home for the children. Even though one of us remained in the family home and maintained the kids' room, all of their furniture, toys and clothing were moved to their mother's new place at the time of separation. Returning to their old room they felt almost as strange as other kids do when they go to their dad's new place. Our kids remarked about the confusion, at first, of having two places. "Sometimes I'd wake up and forget where I was."

There was fear associated with a new place as well. One six-year-old could not sleep alone in a new bedroom for several months. She would invariably crawl into her mother or father's bed in the middle of the night. In retrospect she was able to laugh while describing the bogeyman who lived in the closet of the room. It seemed that all the fears of the new home, the divorce, and the uncertain future culminated in that dark unfamiliar room in the dead of night. The shadowy accumulation of all her worries, the bogeyman, was going to get her.

Integrating their two homes, especially one where there were few obvious or familiar amusements at first, was a problem. "It was so boring at Dad's house. There was nothing to do," said seven-year-old Jennifer. "If Dad didn't do things with me and if Kathryn (her sister) was reading, I'd play hide-and-seek with the dog." And her dog is about as phlegmatic a partner for that sort of game as ever walked on four (or two) feet.

Getting used to a new neighborhood and making new friends won't happen overnight. And it may be difficult for a father to help pave the way for his kids. Usually, when a family moves into a new neighborhood, the mother gets acquainted with other mothers first. Even in these liberated times, there are still more mothers than fathers taking care of children in a neighborhood during the middle of the day. And the mothers may have had more practice, already, at breaking the ice for their kids.

The Shepard kids mentioned that their dad's apartment—the first child-sharing environment—was grim. They were not able to meet any kids, and generally were out of sorts socially when they were with their dad. However, a move to a friendly area with more kids, a bigger house, and a generally more regularized routine made them feel better. But it was hard for them to leave their friends after school or during a weekend to go to a new place where they did not know anyone.

## CHILD-SHARING ARRANGEMENTS

We asked our kids what they thought of the child-sharing arrangement. They responded by citing some of the on-going characteristics of living in two homes. The adjustments which they were required to make to their parents as two independent adults were instructive. We boggle at the thought of being asked to make some of these adjustments ourselves.

First came packing. They said they got tired of packing every week, and admonished us for being angry if they forgot something. We agreed. Even Marco Polo must have gotten pissed at having to pack and repack. Our kids (and yours) are a lot younger than he was and they're not going to meet the great Khan; they're only going to stay at your house.

But the kids also said that the packing exercise helped them take better care of themselves. We believe that the packing contributes to the kids becoming independent and responsible people. While we wouldn't recommend divorcing so that the kids could pack every week, neither of us is too regretful about riding the kids (not unmercifully) when they don't bring the things they know they will need. In truth, there were not many times that they were lax. They probably didn't even need our prodding to see that a forgotten sweater or underwear makes more of a problem for them than Dad's nagging.

The kids from both families laughed a lot (and not altogether joyfully) when they talked about the food cooked at each parent's home. They cited instances of going from their mom's to their dad's house and getting spaghetti on two successive nights. This stimulated a discussion about the need to adjust to each parent's moods and requirements.

Often, now that the parents don't live together, their parents' requirements of them are different. Dad makes you pick up your things immediately after finishing with them. Mom does a general cleaning once a week. One parent may be stricter about clearing the table or bedtime than the other. The kids said they had to remember two sets of rules and which parent had which rules. This took time. If this is Tuesday, I've got to make my bed, eat all my vegetables and feed the dog. If it's Wednesday, I've got to take off my shoes in the hall and put my dirty clothes near the washer.

While neither of us has the problem in the extreme, we have friends who are divorced and who adopted radically varied lifestyles after separation. During marriage many strong individual personality traits are submerged by each partner for the sake of the marriage. When the couple splits, these traits reemerge, and sometimes more powerfully for having been dammed up for so long. One parent may become a strict vegetarian and demand that the kids eat no meat when they are at either parent's house. This must exacerbate the burden on their children of adjusting to each parent, especially when the children are actively involved with both parents.

Our only advice here is to try to separate lifestyle from parental concern and love. The kids understand what our major demands as fathers are. We don't ask them to carry these over to their mothers' homes. An oft-heard statement with many variations is, "This is the way we'll live when we live together here (my house). You will have to do as your mom asks when you live with her." We believe that exposure to several ways of living will not harm our children. If the lifestyles are not presented in a dogmatic way, our kids can live them and use them to develop their own identities as they mature. We also believe that presenting one lifestyle as the only way to live, and then requiring your kids to spend a part of their childhood in what you or their mother clearly defines as an undesirable life setting, can be harmful. As we have said in other parts of this book, you and your former wife are two important models for helping your kids develop their personalities. You can present the models and help them make choices. But ramming one particular model down their throats will very rarely convert them to it.

Our kids perceived the divorce as helping their family make a fresh start. It had a positive effect on their relationships with their parents. They said that each parent paid more attention to them. They received more interaction. ("When you see your mom after three days of being with your dad, you get more hugs and kisses because you missed each other.")

The kids felt that they did more things with each parent than they did as a total family prior to the separation. However, more activities with their parents may be due in part to the kids getting older and being able to participate in a wider range of experiences.

What advice would our kids give to other kids whose parents are divorced? It takes time to work out all the problems; between kids and their two homes, between the former husband and wife as parents. But it can work out. And in many ways it can be better than before.

We have not identified clearly the phases of adjustment which our kids have undergone. But talking with them about their past and present has helped us to see how much of an adjustment we are asking them to make and how well they responded. There was no magic involved in helping our kids over some very rough places in their young lives. The major factor was active contact with them by both ourselves and our former wives.

Viewed in allegorical terms, our kids and we have been on a long hike. (If the hike weren't voluntary, we would have to call it a forced march.) When we came to some very rough terrain, our kids would have dropped out if we and our former wives had not taken them by the hand and escorted them through it. They couldn't go on by themselves. Sometimes we had to carry them. But they soon realized that at least one of us would be there when they needed us during the rockiest places. The road is still rough, but our kids can move with us a bit more independently now. And they know they can count on us if they need us.


## THEIR CONCERNS AND FEARS

In summary, what were the things which concerned the kids most? At the top of the list was environment, next came food, then logistics, closely followed by rules. Their hierarchy of concern may be surprising, but it is rational. Prior to the divorce the Shepard kids lived in the hills near Berkeley, California. They were then transplanted to a Boston suburb in the middle of the winter. Their dad's apartment was not comparable to the Berkeley Hills house which overlooked the Golden Gate Bridge and San Francisco Bay. Now they had to live with (or visit, for the first few months) their dad in the bottom half of a two-family house which overlooked a lot of other similar houses. Their introduction to the East Coast was in February; it was cold and their dad's new apartment had a double bed mattress on the floor. When you walked around the other rooms there was a tremendous echo. A lot of divorced, middle-aged, middle-class fathers are social skidders, at least during the first stages, and so was the Shepard dad. It took him almost a year to get beds and towels and dishes, and he never did get curtains at the windows in the two years he lived there. Thus it could be expected that the Shepard kids, when asked to be reflective about divorce, would say their dad's apartment was "boring." And they hated that part of it.

If you are a middle-class (most of us are, or at least we call ourselves so) divorced dad, you will want to remember that your kids may not like to see you during your social skidding period. There is nothing as cold and unrelenting as an apartment without furniture. And do not let anyone tell you that with bare floors and little or no furniture you can relate to your children in the same way that you did in your adequately furnished house. We have talked to dozens of divorced dads, and even those whose wives had moved out of the house felt an immediate decrease in their standard of living. The kids don't like it.

"Hot dogs and Gatorade," said the Shepard children when queried about their father's culinary skills. Actually, that menu was only served twice, but given a divorced dad's lack of cash and low cooking skill level, hot dogs are usually part of the fare. When kids are used to well-prepared and nutritionally balanced meals, little wonder they would rank food next to environment on the scale of things that bothered them most after the divorce.

Fortunately, you can learn to cook. Start with something simple but stay away from prepared foods (TV dinners and the like). They are costly and contain too many empty calories. Food is important, not just nutritionally but because it is at mealtime that you can talk to each other and generally feel like a family again. Kids are concerned about food. Indeed, one of the Shepard kids often stays an extra day with one of his parents if he knows the other is having something for dinner that he doesn't like. Or he calls in advance to see if the menu planning is nearing completion so he can adjust his schedule. Neither parent lets him do it often these days, though it took a while to figure out the abrupt changes in his visiting schedule.

We both knew that the kids would mention something about logistics. In the early stages they were all fractious about packing and remembering how many pairs of underpants, stockings and other articles were needed. Also, the logistics became complicated in part because of the social skidding syndrome; the mother had a washer and dryer, so dirty clothes had to be transported. (Laundromats are grim. They take a lot of time. You stand there fighting with a battered Maytag that rejects foreign and American coins, and then suddenly picture the gleaming appliances nestled side by side in your ex-wife's home. It can make you pretty grouchy.)

Some of the logistics are solvable (two sets of toothbrushes, etc.), but no one can afford two sets of clothes. We pay more for our kids' sneakers than we pay for our own, and they can wear out three or four pairs each year.

Next came the rules. When we were married we did not realize how different our wives' rules were from our own. Both the Goldman and Shepard youngsters cited differences. They did not say things were radically different, but enough so that they had to remember at whose house they were. Sometimes the kids cited simple things,

119

like Dad was neater than Mom, or less strict about the TV. Then they consciously thought about when and how they could bend the rules a little and about who was likely to be strict on what issue. Becoming aware of all these calculations gives you a good idea of what kids' lives are like in a child-sharing arrangement. We realize that they have to shift gears a lot, but in the long run that may not be detrimental. It does sharpen their skills in social analysis and, given their ability to shove three days' clothes in their backpacks within three minutes, they could be trained for disaster relief teams easily. So, our idea is that the packing, rule assessing, and change of nutrition may not be all that bad. It may even make them more employable.

# 8
## *You and Your Children Outside the Family*

The prevalent view of America is that we are a kid-oriented society. However, we have enough serious doubts about that view to suggest that divorced dads had better pay special attention to three areas: the kids' schools and education, their cultural enrichment, and their health and nutrition. We are not implying that their mother is not also responsible for insuring that the kids get a good start in life. Rather we believe that it takes two parents— particularly when there has been a divorce.

Why special attention? Most married dads are not involved in selecting cultural or educational activities for their kids. Furthermore, when we were married we were not actively involved in any of the three areas. Thus we have had to retrain ourselves. In the process we have learned that a divorced dad had better be vigilant if he wants his kids to be able to read and write, to be active members of society, and to appreciate and participate in music, just to mention a few areas of their development.

As a married father, you probably met with your kids' teachers less than your wife did. When it came to such activities as piano lessons, summer camps, art school, or dance lessons, your wife probably did the research and made the necessary contacts. Sure, she consulted you. And you reacted, first, by asking how much it was going to cost; second, by grumbling that this was the unforeseen item which would break the budget's back; and finally, by not being able to say no because maybe the kid was a latent Pablo Picasso or Margot Fonteyn, and you knew the importance of encouraging creative talent at an early age. And, if your marriage was even remotely traditional, your wife handled the health and nutrition department. Maybe you could shop and cook, but she knew more about it so you let her do it.

When you are sharing your children with your former wife, you can't leave all these considerations to her. Now that the marriage no longer exists, each former partner must do the total cycle of caring for themselves and their kids. Unless she is financially independent, your ex-wife will have a job. Her time will be taken up with all the life-sustaining tasks (find a plumber, get the car fixed, get the cat spayed) which you formerly shared. Even with the best of intentions she may not be able to take care of the kids' special needs with the consummate skill and efficiency she provided during your marriage. You will have to be more active. Aside from the benefits your increased participation will yield for your kids, your new interest in these areas of their lives will bring you closer to them. It is a way of further enhancing your involvement with them.

122

# SCHOOLS AND EDUCATION

Your children's education is the primary stimulus for what they will do with the rest of their lives. The more horizons opened for them in school, the more options they will explore as they grow and the more confidently they will seek training later when it's time to earn a living.

How do you know what the quality of their education is? Are they being educated at all? What role do you play in insuring that their education is adequate? Are they reading at grade level? Do they have the requisite mathematical skills?

Your kids spend more time in schools than they do in any other single institution. For this reason alone you need to pay close attention to what is happening to them. This will not be easy because schools— especially public ones—do not like dealing with fathers. Our experience is that they do not like having conferences with more than one parent, particularly if the second is a divorced dad.

This is how the public schools usually go about their business. They send a single, ill-typed, poorly written and illegibly printed message that something important is going to occur to your child. They expect the mother to respond, and if you and your kids are not getting together the day the school epistle arrives, then you will be in the dark about what is happening. The event will pass you by because you are not in the communication link. How do you get there?

The first thing is to make sure your former wife and kids will make every effort to keep you informed. Next, it should be on the school records that your youngsters have two homes. Some schools will give you a hard time about this, but persevere. They should have you listed as a parent and should be aware of their obligation to keep you informed.

123

You should also make a big push to see each one of your kids' teachers. This is especially important for divorced dads. If some teachers (and schools) discover that a student's parents are divorced and they do not meet both of the parents, they will assume that the parents (and particularly the father) do not care about their kids. If this happens the squeaky-wheel-gets-the-grease law applies. Given the number of students in each classroom, a teacher can ignore apparently passive parents and focus on the vocal and active ones. Sad, but we found it to be true. Worse, when there is some problem, the kid does not receive the best treatment.

For example, the youngest Shepard child did not like kindergarten in New England. His previous experience had been a wild and wooly, exciting private school in Berkeley, California, that concentrated on freedom as a major educational goal. As might be expected, when Aaron Shepard arrived in a small suburban Boston school to find that kindergarten during February consisted of a lot of singing and playing ring-around-the-rosey, he was not ecstatic about being there.

After several bad weeks Aaron told his parents he did not intend to continue—he was dropping out of kindergarten. And this he did. No one could convince him—not even a number of discussions with a young, personable school principal.

The result of Aaron's recalcitrant behavior toward this school was that they decreed he was dyslexic and so immature that he would have to repeat kindergarten.

Aaron's mother met several times with the school faculty and received the same diagnosis. In the interim his father took him to an independent evaluator/tester and gathered some objective data about Aaron's capabilities. Armed with the independent data the father returned to the public school for a meeting.

When presented with an independent assessment that Aaron was not at all dyslexic, and a bright child to boot, they—the teacher, principal, and a counselor—all agreed that his dislike of kindergarten was due to divorce. An escalation of causes—if a kid does not do well in school and the school cannot prove genetic or birth-related deficiencies, they then turn to a less serious physical or mental one. If that does not prove to be the case, then they go for social and familial causes. As it turns out, Aaron was bored with their view of education, but they never considered that possibility.

The major lesson here is that most of the institutions which are supposed to be helping kids will focus on the divorce or some other problem not related to school as the center of all perceived and real problems. However, if the divorced dad (in concert with his former wife) is paying attention, he might be able to get at the real causes. If he is not participating in his children's lives, there is a very good chance that the schools will make unwarranted assumptions.

As the major institution in your child's life, the school poses other problems. The biggest ones are, of course, logistics and learning. If your former wife lives in a town different from yours, and you are sharing your child regularly, this means a lot of driving. The kids will stay at your house and go to school in another town. The only way this works out over a long period of time is if your former wife helps. She has to share some of the driving. Next is the problem with learning. Not only do kids conveniently forget their homework (left at their mother's), but they also can avoid telling you they are having trouble. So you have to be patient when they forget and ever-vigilant about making sure that they know the basic skills. They will tell you they did their homework at their mother's. Maybe they did, but you have to ask and check. It takes *two* involved parents to insure that kids will get what they need to operate in our society.

Make it a point, then, to ask and assess how the kids are doing on a week-by-week basis. Teacher conferences are always held at the convenience of teachers and mother/housewives. Therefore, if you attend you will find the teachers amazed, dismayed, or even shocked. In our experience, fathers at teacher's conferences are about as welcome as a pregnant pole vaulter at a track meet. However, you will find teachers being much more direct with a dad and less likely to pawn off some hokum. The public schools have a long way to go before realizing that most moms are not simple-minded, and most dads are not more difficult to talk to.

Despite these barriers, as a divorced dad you should meet all of your kids' teachers at least once during the year. You can switch off with your former wife on the regularly scheduled parent-teacher conferences. The children seem to appreciate that both parents are interested in their progress in school. By knowing the children's teachers personally, you will be better able to talk with them about their progress. When your child tells you about some specific event which happened, you can talk more knowledgeably about it with your child if you know the teacher.

It is difficult to earn a living, attend teacher's conferences, and check on homework, but you will have to do all these things. You can't assume that your children are learning basic skills merely because they are receiving passing grades. You have to find out what their grades really mean. In other words you will have to relate their grades to their skills. If, for example, as one divorced dad recently told us, a kid receives all A's but, as a fourth grader, had difficulty reading the headlines, then you will know something is askew. Do not assume things are going well in school. Do not assume that passing or high marks are measures of your kids' acquired skills. Check these things for yourself. If you have any doubts, most universities have testing centers and reading clinics which test and evaluate kids for very little money.

## CULTURAL ENRICHMENT

Exposing your youngsters to special cultural opportunities outside of those offered at school may have a lifelong impact on them. By "cultural opportunities" we are referring to everything from special sports instruction to violin lessons. These activities, begun in childhood, often become important to a person throughout his or her life.

Have you ever played tennis with someone who moved with a grace and fluidity which you could never capture yourself? Have you ever heard a friend play the guitar or piano really well but with simplicity and a minimum of flourishes? The chances are that he or she "has been doing it all his life." In other words, the skill was developed in childhood. And if you didn't begin learning it while still young, you won't capture that effortless grace no matter how good you are at related activities or how proficient you become at the new activity. That kind of seemingly effortless skill can bring a lifetime of satisfaction.

As your kids grow toward adulthood and beyond, they may face times when their effectiveness, competence, or potential for success will be in doubt. Being able to resort to certain lifelong pursuits in which they are competent can add valuable balance to their lives. The vast majority of our children will not be Billie Jean Kings or Isaac Sterns. But who knows? Maybe one of your youngsters will have a special gift. The only way to discover it is to create an environment conducive to its development. Even if you don't create a world champ you can still help your kids get over those dry times in later life when the world looks grey and the only satisfying hours are those spent sketching or picking at the guitar.

Adding new dimensions to the lives of your children is indeed an important reason for helping them acquire a variety of skills. How many times have you seen or heard a bright, healthy youngster (age one to nineteen) say, "I'm bored." That short phrase often signals a parental failure. If a kid in the midst of a middle-class home repeats the slogan many times, what will happen when he or she becomes a teenager or young adult? Cultural activities are aimed at filling the "I'm bored" spots in their lives. They are aimed also at developing discipline, both physical and mental. Standing on a street corner with other bored kids will be far less appealing if your kids have sports abilities or cultural interests.

A suggestion here: you should help them select particular sports and cultural activities which will most likely be beneficial in their later lives. Many of the things they learn in school, especially team sports, have relatively little carryover into adult life. It's tough to keep that batting eye or shooting touch active twenty years out of high school. And then there's always the problem of finding enough people for a good game. So it's important to expose your kids to as many cultural activities as they can and want to absorb. Sometimes they will ask to be involved in a particular activity. That's an easy one. But sometimes you may have to nudge them. Be alert for special inclinations. Does your son bang on the pots and pans when you are preparing dinner? Maybe drum lessons for him. Does your daughter stand on her head whenever anyone will watch her? Maybe gymnastics for her. If your child doesn't take to the suggestion about special lessons enthusiastically or if, after several lessons, the kid isn't really turned on, don't push him or her further. It is best to drop it before the activity becomes a burden for your child.

Like visiting the teacher, you will have to decide which parent sets up the classes and which parent pays. Arranging for classes depends on all your respective schedules; yours, your former wife's and your youngster's. For example, you may want to arrange the class so that your kid can walk to it after school. That may mean that the parent who lives nearest the child's school should find a class in the local neighborhood, if possible.

Should the money for the class come out of support payments? Should it be a shared expense, or should the person making more money pay for it because it is an extra? That's a knotty problem. It should be negotiated and based on both of your expenditures. But payment need not be irrevocable or set in concrete. Perhaps one year it comes out of the support payment and the next year the cost is shared, depending on your respective financial circumstances.

Maybe, after all the talk and planning, neither you or your ex-wife can financially extend yourselves to pay for the lessons. That may be a hard reality. There is no way to take the pain out of not being able to provide all the extras for your kids. Since our society provides us with an almost limitless array of choices, all families face this problem on some level, whatever their income. Our former wives and we have tried to underwrite one special cultural project at a time for each kid. Financially that is all that we can afford. And that is all our kids can absorb at one time, given their school schedule and current needs for other unstructured time.

Despite the fact that Jimmy Connors' mother built him, inch by inch, into a worldbeater, we believe that pushing your kids into these extracurricular activities in any way which borders on the zealous can be harmful. They should be allowed to enjoy the activity and to progress at their own rate. The last thing any of them needs is a lot of pushing to continue an activity in which they have no interest. If they lose interest and want to drop out, let them without making a big deal about it. A ballet teacher told one of us that his daughter had an unusual talent at the same time that she was saying she didn't want to take lessons any more. She dropped it. We have seen too many cases in which kids were forced to stay in these various activities for years but who now don't play the piano, hit a tennis ball, or ride a horse. We can think of few worse human tragedies than an individual being alienated from participating in the very activity in which he has some proficiency because that activity causes him too much emotional pain. And there are many more of these types than there are Jimmy Connors. You just don't read about them.

## HEALTH AND NUTRITION

Creating good health and good health habits is another foundation block for your kids. Good health affects everything, including attitudes, emotions, and relationships with others throughout life. Since part of your role as a parent is to help your kids prepare for the day when they won't need you any more, you will want to feel that you have sent them out into the world in as healthy a state as possible. You know that at some point they will need all the physical and emotional strength they can find.

You and your former wife need to plan jointly for your children's health, at least at first: whose teeth need attention, what doctor is best for the children, who should be called in case of medical emergencies. You both should compare notes carefully about the health insurance programs you are under. If you both work, the chances are that one of you will have a more beneficial or cheaper medical plan which can include your kids. Don't naturally assume that just because you always carried your former wife and your kids on a medical plan at work, you should continue to do so. Hers may cost less or provide better coverage.

One of the nice things about having kids around is that they usually look pretty good. They have shiny hair, attractive bodies, and no wrinkles. And the way to keep them looking good is to feed them well. Your house is the garden; your kids are like growing plants. What you feed them will determine how they bloom, physically. If they create enjoyment for you as a parent, part of that is the visual joy you get from their looking good.

We are far from being nutritionists but we try to think of balancing their diets when they are with us. "What did you have last night at your Mom's house?" We try to fill in any gaps from the day before in the basic fruit, meat, dairy, and vegetable groups. We keep a mental log of what we have been feeding them and try to include some basic food from each of the four categories every day. And while we don't fill them full of sweets, we know that some desserts provide quick energy and won't harm them at the end of a meal. Frozen yogurt can create a lot of wild anticipation.

We have cited already the broad swings in food regimens between two people who are no longer living together. We have mentioned the efforts the kids may have to make in adjusting to each parent's styles and preferences.

Within that context try to tune in on what your kids like to eat. What are their individual preferences? For example, one child may not like meat. You will have to prepare more vegetables with every meal to accommodate that. You will have to know which vegetables provide adequate protein. You may begin to feel like a short-order cook after catering to each individual taste.

Society will not automatically educate your kids or provide them with cultural opportunities. Good medical care will not by itself insure that kids will be healthy. Being on the school baseball team will not necessarily help them keep down their cholesterol levels or weight. The divorced dad and mom have to separately and jointly watch how society's institutions are treating their kids.

# 9
## *How Others Survive*

We believe that the best way we can convince divorced dads to stay close to their kids is to accurately present the successes and failures in our own lives. That has been our primary approach. But in case you are a person who likes to look at "hard data," we offer a summary of recent research on how important fathers and children are to each other. We are not trying to be scientific. We don't think that raising kids and being a divorced father have much to do with science. Rather, they have to do with your emotional well-being and that of your children. But here is some information about what is going on with other divorced fathers and their kids. We're not the only people who believe in your active participation as a parent.

# THE HAPPIEST MAN

Not too long ago one of us participated in a Brandeis University study on divorced fathers. The most important finding from the Brandeis study was that divorced fathers who stay involved with their kids on a regular basis are happier. Given that divorce is one of the most unhappy events of your life, it is noteworthy that you can derive some good out of a bad situation.

Another important finding came from a study done at Harvard. This long-term study about men who went to Harvard was not concerned specifically with divorced dads. Nevertheless, it found that the "happiest" men many decades after graduating from Harvard were those who had received vocational guidance from their fathers. (We hypothesize that this would be true for women, also.) This says to us that, apart from paying for ortho-dontia and clothes, you are an important part of your kids' lives because giving them a sense of how you feel about your work, and giving them guidance about ways in which they can make their own financial way in life will have a lasting effect.

Happiness for yourself; happiness for your kids if you provide them with strong vocational objectives. Sounds simple. Maybe it is. Maybe these studies would prove wrong if they were repeated with larger populations. However, these results from Harvard and Brandeis are worth considering in the context of major social movements.

Your family has broken up and you've spent a lot of time lately thinking about the part that you played in it all. Thoughts of your divorce make you feel like a dirty dog. Well, probably you have been a dirty dog . . . to some extent. And your ex-wife has acted like the female counterpart. But lest you destroy yourself with recrimi-nations and self-flagellation, you should understand that some of the causes of your family's breakup lie outside the sphere of your personal behavior or that of your ex-wife. They are due, in part, to changes in our society.

## CHANGING FAMILY PATTERNS

Marriage was meant to last forever when people lived to age forty or fifty. One hundred years ago, in an agrarian culture, men died at those ages after having worked more than one young wife to death—if the women didn't die in childbirth first. In those days child labor and woman labor were essential for a family's survival. And the institution of marriage protected this economic base.

There have been changes since then. We live longer, we work less or differently; women don't die as often in childbirth; and childrearing, now an option rather than an inevitability, takes at most twenty years out of an increasingly long lifetime (1). For example, a woman who bears the last of two children (the number in the average family) when 25 years old will still be under 40 with two-thirds of her adult life ahead of her by the time the youngest child is fairly self-sufficient. In the past, the age spread was wider (2), and life expectancy much shorter.

Some people say that marriage is becoming obsolete. No longer having socio-economic reasons for existing, it has little *practical* utility (3). And if a marriage, then, is made solely for intimacy, you and your former wife are living members of an army who will attest to the difficulty of sustaining intimacy over a lifetime, or even over a Sunday afternoon. These are some of the factors which now buffet the traditional institution of marriage. Although some evidence makes one feel that the institution is dead or dying (one out of every two and one-half American marriages breaks up; 40% of school-age children live in families without two natural parents), we are not ready to hold a funeral yet.

We believe that the form of marriage has changed. Many current divorces may be due to expectations of marriage based on images handed down from the first few decades of the twentieth century. These images, or the way people believe their marriage should be, do not fit present reality. We believe that marriage will continue to exist but in altered form(s). You, as a divorced dad, whatever your personal responsibility for your divorce, participated in and were affected by the cultural cross-currents which are changing male/female/child relationships and, ultimately, how people unite and raise families.

## TURNING FAILURE AROUND

We began this book by painting a picture of a divorced dad who feels isolated from the rest of society for a variety of reasons. Although we had these feelings at the time of our divorces, and you may have had them too, none of us are total anomalies. We are a major part of a cultural shift, and because of this we are being studied more closely every day. Here are some of the things that researchers are finding out about us.

A relatively recent study (reported by Heatherington, *et al* in *Psychology Today*) of seventy-two middle-class divorced couples with children showed that divorced men and women tend to do better during the first two months after the separation than during the rest of the first year of the separation (4). Despite the feelings that many couples have about how great it will be after the divorce, few experience the hoped-for euphoria which independence promises.

Men whose wives had not worked had the toughest

time organizing their new lives. Their excessive dependence on their former wives to maintain the household when they were married was evident in their inability to maintain their new households adequately, eat regular meals, and keep themselves in clean shirts. They even reported sleeping less regularly than when they were married.

Newly divorced men complained of feelings of rootlessness and homelessness. Many had deep feelings of failure over the breakup of the marriage which carried over into social situations and work. Many reported heightened sexual incompetence.

How does a recently divorced dad act? During the first year there seems to be a big emphasis on altering one's self-image. Clean-shaven types suddenly sprout beards. Brooks Brothers suits and habitually conservative business garb give way to leather jackets and flowered shirts unbuttoned to mid-chest. Moustaches, sideburns, and longer hair are also quite common at the time. The Heatherington report remarked, "This 'hip, Honda and hirsute syndrome' was perhaps part of their frenetic search for a new identity immediately after the divorce; it abated in the second year."

That same study shows evidence that the first year of divorce was the most difficult for both former partners. Toward the end of the first year a large percentage of both men and women studied believed divorce had been a mistake. They also believed, therefore, that just possibly they should have resolved their differences and remained married. However, by the end of the second year, their views changed again because most of them had new intimate relationships which seemed to fill the marriage void.

There were other interesting findings in this study: among them, that divorced fathers were more likely to keep up with the former couple's married friends. They tended to use these social contacts to organize their own time with their kids on visiting days. Divorced dads, according to this report, became more involved with their children during the first few months of the separation than when they were married. But most saw their children "less and less as time passed." However, ten fathers, or 13% of the study sample, became increasingly involved with their kids and reported improved relations.

While there are all sorts of beliefs about one parent in a divorce being the central villain and the other the victim, there did not seem to be much evidence that either parent escaped some injury. During that dreadful first year at least one member of each family in the study reported a great deal of stress. In time they learned to cope, but the process was not easy. The study concludes that divorced dads feel better and more competent after two years of separation, but they have continuing feelings of rootlessness. Even after two years, many have not completely overcome the divorce. Does that description sound familiar? Compare it then to the following study completed at Brandeis University.

The study was based on interviews with 127 divorced fathers of children aged three to seven. As we mentioned before, one of us was part of the Brandeis study sample. As a means of encouraging divorced dads to participate in similar efforts, we will recount the experience.

The study was advertised on the bulletin board of the company where we worked. Shepard read the advertisement, clipped the number to telephone and then made the call. At the other end of the telephone was an answering service which made an appointment. Within a few weeks a young man appeared at the Shepard residence and asked a series of questions. It was all very painless. In fact, it was interesting because each participant received a summary of the results and therefore was able to identify with a large group of other men having similar experiences with their kids and new relationships with women.

## SUNDAY HERO VS. EVERYDAY FATHER

Most of the Brandeis study fathers were white, middle-class and in their thirties (5). The study divided the dads into four groups: those who spent full time with their kids; those who spent half time with their kids; those who saw their kids on weekends; and those who saw their kids a few times each month. The researchers claim that theirs is the only American study involving direct interviews with fathers since 1956 (6).

From the responses received, men who actively participate in taking care of their kids "develop a stronger self-image . . . and are more expressive emotionally. They claim to have a better understanding of their children and even report that they are now more attractive to women."

The more involved a divorced dad was with his kids, the more at variance he felt with the stereotypical image of the American male. The Brandeis report further found, in a controlled study, what many of us divorced dads have felt as we battled our loneliness and tried, without much reinforcement from the people around us, to work out a reasonable way of not being estranged from our kids. As we pointed out earlier it is hard not to feel like an anomaly when there are no easily seen examples of other people dealing effectively with conditions in life which are similar to yours. The study tells us that there are a lot of divorced dads who feel this way. But they need not; they are part of a rapidly expanding group.

Accordingly, the father who shares his kids, halftime,

is the happiest of the four types. He has fewer conflicts with his ex-wife and feels better about being a father again (7).

Taking care of a child only part of the time complicates a divorced dad's life. Most men found new mates, although those who cared for their children full time had the least active sex lives. Generally the new mates were single and childless. Quarter-time, or weekend, fathers found new partners among divorced mothers.

On the professional front it was found that careers were less important for divorced dads who were actively involved with their kids. The next Brandeis study finding may be the most sobering, if you believe as we do that dads and kids are an important part of our society. It seems as though the higher a father goes up the ladder of success, the less he is involved with his kids. Not surprised? No, we weren't either, but when it appears as a finding of an objective study, it certainly gives one pause. Does it have to be a choice: either career or family? Unfortunately, it probably does for a divorced dad who wants to be one of the world's movers and shakers. However, if you can curb your upwardly mobile impulses and take a realistic view of your chances at "making it," you will be able to make a better choice with respect to your children. Whichever you do—climb up the career ladder or reach out to your kids—make sure you have thought about the consequences.

Since you will not be with your kids as a live-in father every day, you will be increasingly concerned about the quality of time you spend with them. It may be that you will have to make some career choices at some point. We have held out the possibility of adopting a "cottage industry" approach to your job. But this may not work for you. We can only say that we have seen or heard about a lot of married men who leave their kids (and wives) behind as they pursue their careers. It may be a dominant characteristic of our culture. It is a choice one makes, if confronted with this opportunity, whether married or divorced.

The typical half-time father interviewed in the Brandeis study has one child, a boy. The dad has complete responsibility for him every other week or every three and one-half days. The dad lives near his ex-wife. This means the child stays at the same neighborhood school. He does not lose his friends no matter which house he's in. Both houses have the kid's toys and clothes. The half-time father may actually be with his kid about the same amount as a quarter-time dad, but the half-time arrangement seems to make him feel more secure as a father (8).

## THE BENEFITS TO KIDS, DAD, AND SOCIETY

Dads who are actively involved in sharing their children may be doing themselves, as well as their kids, a favor. That involvement may contribute to a sense of stability for both after the disruptive experience of the divorce. According to other recent research, the optimum situation, not only for divorced dads but for all other family members, seems to be when both parents share the child care relatively equally.

We have already described our child-sharing arrangements. But many other arrangements have been reported. One divorced California family has a rigid child-sharing scheme. Every Wednesday the kids eat breakfast in one parent's house and then go to the other's until Sunday morning. At that time they change houses again. Both houses under this arrangement have full sets of clothes and toys. The parents have joint legal custody and find their Wednesday-to-Sunday arrangements work fine (9).

Another cosmopolitan couple has developed a variation of the child-changing-houses routine, reported in *The New York Times*. During their marriage this New York couple spent a lot of time and energy refurbishing an apartment. Their kids love it. So, the two parents each moved to new dwellings and on a predetermined schedule, they move in and out of their kids' home. It seems as though both parents wanted their kids to be happy, even to the tune of supporting three abodes.

Given these variations on the theme of couples sharing their children and the findings of the various studies, questions are no doubt being raised in your mind. How do parents begin thinking about such complicated arrangements? Our experience, the studies of single families, and larger surveys all seem to point to the father. He generally raises the possibility. In a divorce the mother generally assumes that the kids will remain with her even when she believes her ex-husband will remain a significant part of the kids' lives.

The child-sharing conversation probably goes something like this. "What about the kids?"

"Well, they can be with me during the week," says the mother.

"Hell, no, that means I'd only be a weekend dad," replies the dad. "Why not reverse it? They stay with me during the week. You never liked getting up early. I always get them off to school anyway."

"That's unacceptable to me," retorts the mother (10).

Conversations of this sort no doubt go on daily across the country among those parents about to be divorced. But after parents discover that they have a right to share the kids and that the "tender years" doctrine should be abandoned, things will go a little smoother. However, you have to realize that joint custody and child sharing don't create any new emotional bonds. If you are a divorced parent, kids are the only glue.

## VIEW FROM ANOTHER COUNTRY

We'll throw in one other reported child-sharing example because it sheds light from a different direction. It demonstrates the importance which another culture places on being an active father.

The Swedish government has a program which guarantees about 95% of the husband/father's salary while he stays home for up to seven months after the birth of a child. The program does not require the husband to use all seven months, "he can use only part of it; if his wife also works, the two are free to split the time to suit their own needs" (11). If the child is not the firstborn, the father can be with his kids full time for over half a year without worrying about paying the bills. This is the flip side of maternity leave.

If a child's personality is set during the first few years, as many child development professionals believe, then inter-action with the father in these early months would seem to be extremely important. The most socially progressive nation in the world has recognized this and is taking action.

"What we discovered in the early 1970s," said Birget Arve-Pares, a member of the Swedish government's Commission on Family Aid, "was the phenomenon of the 'divorced man,' the husband who found himself psychologically separated, who had lost contact with the realities in which children grow up" (12).

Approximately 7% of eligible fathers now use the program. The percentage has increased each year even though there is evidence that many men would like to take this leave but are fearful for their jobs.

The major finding here is that one may not even have to be divorced to feel cut off from one's children. But there are alternatives for keeping involved with them. Although you may feel that you are swimming against the current, you are not alone. One of the vital points made in the article on child sharing/paternity leave was that the fathers came to value their time with their kids because it helped them to see the world from another perspective. "When you look at it carefully, society is really built for grown-ups. There are more roads than trees, more big cars than little bicycles, more parking lots than playgrounds" (13).

The Brandeis study stated that upward career mobility automatically seemed to move fathers away from their children. The program in Sweden is a way of addressing this problem. While Sweden has its own social problems and life is not perfect over there, our American society has not begun to deal with issues such as these. That is why, every once in a while, it's helpful to step back from one's own culture to gain perspective. Despite the few models available to divorced dads in this country, people here and in other cultures understand that being involved with one's kids is of primary importance in determining what one can do with one's life.


## HOW THE CHILDREN GROW

What about the kids themselves? How do they do with or without their dads? We have found some recent information which supports our personal experiences that active fathering is very important for kids. First, the depressing news. At the Harvard Medical School and the University of Massachusetts, unsettling evidence is emerging. Researchers are discovering that the "absence or inaccessibility of one or both parents" may be important variables in a number of psychiatric problems. However, divorce or death are not the only ways in which absence or inaccessibility come about. Indeed, job demands and aloofness may also be significantly related to these problems of kids (14).

The studies which led to the findings took more than eight years. They focused on Harvard dropouts and patients admitted to mental hospitals. In both cases those groups of individuals who suffered from schizophrenia, withdrawal from the world and the inability to tell fantasy from reality, had experienced (more than twice as much as others) the loss of a parent through death. In other words one characteristic which distinguishes a group of schizophrenics from a control group is that many more of the mentally disturbed persons have lost a parent through death in their early years. The researchers believe that "close warm contact with both parents especially in the first three years of life (is important) to a child's future emotional health."

Dr. Armand Nicholi of the Harvard Medical School, one of the researchers, stated that current trends in American society point to even less contact between parent and child in the future. In comparing the American culture with Russia, where both parents commonly work, but where studies show that parents spend one or two hours a day alone with their kids, he stated, "How many American fathers spend two hours a day alone with their children?"

Dr. Nicholi and his colleague, Dr. Norman Watt of the University of Massachusetts, point to the declining amount of time parents spend with their children and compare this to the ever-increasing divorce, crime, and delinquency rates. They believe that working parents have an extremely difficult time balancing their jobs and attention to their children's needs, but that parents must make an *"unshakeable commitment to make the time available and to listen, not just talk, to their children."*

A complementary study yields a brighter but essentially similar outlook on the importance of fathers staying involved with their children. Stepchildren are as contented and happy as children living with both their natural parents, finds Dr. Paul Bohannan of the University of California. The study covered 1,764 families in San Diego County. In the families where stepfathers were present, the children were happy, satisfied, and without any real father–child problems. The study indicated that it was extremely important to have a father, whether he is natural or a stepfather. The study also showed that stepfathers feel a bit inadequate in their role; they don't believe that they are doing as good a job as the study's results indicate (15). The story of Hansel and Gretel probably set back the credibility of stepparents by about three centuries.

We interpret this information as underscoring the value of a dad in a kid's life. *Even in less than ideal circumstances, having an active father pays off for children.* And surely it has similar benefits for the dads. There is a wide variety of options as to how you can stay involved with your kid once divorced. Whatever option you choose, we have compiled some guidelines based on our experiences and the information we have examined.

## REFERENCES

1. Callahan, Jean, "Why Are All Marriages Breaking Up," *Mother Jones,* July 1977, p. 18.
2. Reinhold, Robert, "The Trend Toward Sexual Equality: Depth of Transformation Uncertain," *The New York Times,* November 30, 1977, p. 24.
3. Callahan, op. cit, p. 18.

4. Heatherington, E., Cox, M. and Cox, R., "Divorced Fathers," *Psychology Today*, April 1977, pp. 42-46.
5. Keshet, H. and Rosenthal, K., "Fathering After Marital Separation," Brandeis University Study, Waltham, Ma., 1978, p. 1.
6. Dullea, Georgia, "Divorced Fathers: Who Are Happiest?," *The New York Times*, February 3, 1978, p. 20.
7. Ibid., p. 20.
8. Ibid., p. 20.
9. Kellogg, Mary, "Life/Style," *Newsweek*, January 24, 1977.
10. Baum, Charlotte, "The Best of Both Parents," *The New York Times Magazine*, October 31, 1976.
11. Semple, Robert B., Jr., "Seven Months with the New Baby," *The New York Times*, December 9, 1976, p. 55.
12. Ibid., p. 85.
13. Ibid., p. 85.
14. Bruzelius, Nils J., "Impact of Losing a Parent Researched," *The Boston Globe*, June 7, 1976.
15. Associated Press, "Study Finds Stepchildren Content," *The New York Times*, November 28, 1976.

# 10
## *Guidelines: From Fast Food Father to Everyday Dad*

We have given you a lot of "nuts and bolts" advice about how to stay actively involved with your kids. You do not have to start working immediately on all the areas we have outlined. In the same way that you can't set up your home to accommodate your kids all at once, in a puff of smoke, addressing all the issues we have raised will take time. It has taken us collectively over fifteen years to gain this experience. And neither of us would say that we are on top of it all yet. Quite the contrary.

Starting in one area will carry over and affect many others. For example, when you begin to include your kids in preparing the meals, you will be moving into the areas of health and nutrition. They will see how certain foods are selected and prepared. They will ask you why you are cooking with vegetable oil instead of butter, and you will explain about food which may be harmful to the arteries and heart, invoking Mr. Cholesterol from the TV commercial. Involving them in preparing the food sets the stage for their assuming greater skill and responsibility for themselves in other areas, gaining confidence through accomplishment, and taking some of the child care load off you.

At other times they will not ask you. But they will adopt some of your habits and realize many years later that they have never questioned the way they stock up on food, or fold their clothes, or keep the bathroom clean. They will realize that there are dozens of alternatives for doing each task, and they may then approach it differently. But you got them to the point where they could decide and choose on the basis of their own health and good judgment.

There are some basic rules which we would like to leave with you. They summarize our experiences and thoughts. More importantly, we believe that they are basic guidelines to approaching a healthy divorced dad/kid relationship. Before you begin taking action in any area of your children's lives, keep them in mind.

1. *Develop custody arrangements early.*

When you are just beginning to separate from your wife, start discussing what sort of arrangements you want to make with respect to the kids. This is much more important than worrying about your property. You don't need to have every detail described on the day you leave, but you do have to have a general understanding about how you want to share your children.

We realize this may sound too rational. One of us had this general understanding and the other didn't. It may not be possible for a divorced dad to make the arrangements during the early stages. If that happens to you, if you are not clear about what you want, then don't do anything which may preclude your having a regular relationship with your kids. In other words, don't sign away your rights. Don't agree to giving their mother sole custody if you are not sure what you want. Be careful during the early stages; make sure you have given yourself enough time to think about what you want before you even visit an attorney.

It is also very important when you do find an attorney to make sure he doesn't give you a fast shuffle. He may not like your arrangements, particularly if they involve joint custody. Don't be intimidated by an attorney. He is to facilitate what you want, and you should not try to fit your problems into an attorney's timeworn preconceived solutions. Remember, you are the buyer. Shop around for an attorney who can help you with your ideas about how to be with your children.

2. *Don't be a Disneyland Dad.*

We have said it in many ways. Your kids need to know you as a real person, not as a visiting hero. Raising children is one of the most complex and important tasks you will face in your life. In order to do it well you must be in tune with what your kids are feeling and thinking. You won't do it well if you see your kids sporadically and under artificial circumstances. Let your kids into your life. Get into theirs. Try to create time and space for each other.

You can be a Disneyland Dad while married and living with your family. Many of the props provided by our society to help kids overcome their problems (shrinks, after school programs, hot lines) are there because parents, married or divorced, don't pay enough attention to their kids. If you spend time with your children, sharing your life with them, you'll have less need of the props. And your kids will survive the divorce.

3. *Remember, your kids see you as a model.*

Often the reason that people say a child is the "spitting image" of a parent is not only because of similar physical appearances. Consciously and subconsciously, the child has adopted the parent's mannerisms. This carries over into lifetime behavior. It's not just in the way they walk and the way they use their hands when talking. It reflects attitudes, outlook, and the way your kids will treat other people when they are independent adults. Children make a lot of your behavior part of themselves. So, think about what you do.

4. *Keep your appointments.*

The divorce complicates the patterns of all family members. Aside from the more obvious complications, logistics become a larger issue. There are two homes. One can no longer be expected to turn up eventually at one central place. There is more fragmentation in everyone's life.

In order to build confidence in your children that the divorce will not continue to disrupt their lives, you should be where you say you will be, on time, every time. You should expect the same from your former wife and kids.

5. *Develop a plan.*

If you believe that active involvement with your kids is best attained by consistent contact with them, you will need a plan. Now that your family is living under more than one roof, each family member is more likely to go his or her separate way without the other members knowing about it. Rightly so. When you add the unpredictability of the weather and other intervening events into the equation, it will be difficult to get together with your kids, consistently, if there is no plan. Rather than planning your time with your kids around the other events in your or your former wife's life, other activities should be planned around the schedule you have developed to be with your kids. It is the only way that you will be able to maintain consistency with them.

We have presented several plans in the body of the book. Each divorced family's plan will differ according to the family members' needs. Try not to move toward more child sharing than you can handle reasonably. *Don't do too much too soon.* If you have just separated and are living in one furnished room far on the other side of town from your former wife and kids, an equal child-sharing arrangement where the kids are with you half the week may be more than you or they can handle. A single overnight at that point may be best. You can plan for the next stage when you will be more settled, your surroundings will be able to accommodate your kids better, and the logistics of getting the kids to and from their school will be worked out. The plan need not be set rigidly. It can change as your life circumstances change.

6. *Keep your youngsters out of the battles between you and your former wife.*

You can keep the kids' involvement in the battles with your former wife to a minimum. Try to get your former wife to agree to hold discussions about finances, property, lawyers, and any other potentially explosive subjects at times other than when you are meeting to exchange the children. Talk with her, not only about your child-sharing intentions, but also about the need for you both to transcend whatever problems you have with each other whenever the welfare of the kids is concerned.

There are reasons for this. The less you argue when the children are around, the less they will feel somehow responsible for the breakup of the marriage. Child sharing will mean that you and your former wife will have to discuss plans for the children more often. It will not be effective if you battle when you are making arrangements for or discussing the well-being of the kids. It would be quite unrealistic to expect that any formerly married couple will never express their anger with each other. The first years of divorce almost always entail a process of working that anger through. And it is healthy to be able to express it directly. But pick the time and the place. Try to keep it from involving your kids. You and your former wife can bring the best sides of yourselves to bear where your children are concerned.

7. *Watch for signs that your kids need special attention.*

Your children may be having difficulty adjusting to the divorce or to other problems in their lives. Be alert for signs of this, but try not to read too much into any one specific event. Repeated trouble in a specific area will tell you that your child may be having a problem. *One* wet bed or *one* neighbor's broken window is still merely an accident.

School performance is a helpful indicator of how your kids are doing. The two points to check at school are: are they working up to potential, whatever that potential may be; how are they developing socially? Active involvement with your kids means that you will check on their performance with the teacher one or more times each year. The teacher will give you an objective impression, in most cases, which you can compare with your own and other comments of significant people in their lives.

If you believe one of your youngsters needs special attention, try first to resolve the problem by being the first source of this attention. Take some extra time to talk over what seem to be the main issues. Try to work out a plan with your child in which you are involved as a close and supportive part of the plan.

If you cannot resolve the problem through your own special participation, you may have to seek outside help. But remember, no one knows your kids as well as you. And your kids have more confidence in you and your former wife than in any other adult in the world. Many problems would evaporate if parents paid more attention to them. Seeking outside help is a serious step and one which should be taken only after you and your former wife have determined that neither of you can possibly turn the situation around.

8. *Help your children feel at home in your house.*

One of the most important parts of having your kids at your home on a regular basis is that they feel comfortable there. Of course, you have to tell them "this is your second home," and behave accordingly. However, you have to do more than talk to them about it.

They will feel at home in your house when they understand the neighborhood, and particularly when they get to know the other kids. You can help them establish new friendships.

When you play outdoors near your home with your kids you are very likely to attract other children. You can facilitate introductions when this occurs. Or you can invite some of the neighborhood kids over for a birthday party.

Whatever your method, helping find friends for your kids at your new place is probably the most important thing you can do in making them feel at home.

9. *Be deliberate about getting a plan operating.*

Child sharing is a fluid process. It will take time to reach a stage where you and your children feel comfortable with it.

It will take time to put all the pieces into place. Creating an environment for your kids in your home takes time. When you are divorced, financial extras don't come easy. And the extra beds and bedding for your kids were not items planned in your budget. Neither were toys or the extra food you will buy if your children stay with you for several days each week. You don't have to do it all in one day or month. In fact, sharing the experience of doing it with your kids is a good way of spending time with them.

Creating an environment for your children is more than tangible objects in their room or space. You and they will have to become comfortable with the child-sharing arrangements. And this takes time as well. It will take time to understand how many days in each parent's home is best for them. It will take time for them to resolve any fears or confusion they might have about moving back and forth between the two homes. And, if you have been a Disneyland Dad in the past, it will take time for your kids to understand and value the new routine. Take it a step at a time. You can't do it all at once.

# Epilogue

We have tried to muster all the personal and anecdotal information we could to argue for having divorced fathers stay involved with their kids. That information was derived from our experiences as divorced dads. However, we have some additional thoughts which are more related to another part of our lives—our experiences as social policy analysts.

Each of us, for more than a decade, has been evaluating and administering children's services. We were both involved as senior level managers in the War on Poverty (which had a significant kid focus). Recently we drafted new legislation for Massachusetts to improve its social services to children and their families. Based on these and other related experiences, we know that a divorced dad cannot abandon or ignore his children in the hope that some governmental or private program will fill the gap.

Foster homes, day care services, counselors, and boarding schools are some of the traditional institutions you might think that, along with one parent, might be able to take care of your kids. However, it just isn't happening. These services, when they are fully funded and well run (which isn't often) are a poor substitute for a mother and father. We simply have not found *any* institution which does as well for a kid as his parents. Also, it is important to note that we are not alone in these views.

There are increasing examples of kids who have been deemed predelinquent or delinquent or have been removed from their homes. Often they are sent to some sort of group care or foster home, or to a larger, more impersonal place. Then they often become runaways. A number of social workers have told us that these kids will run away to their homes. Often these homes are unfit because one or both parents have significant physical or personal problems. Yet these kids run away . . . home. Even an alcoholic or depressed parent offers more love and nurturing than the currently available alternatives. Thus, social workers are less likely to remove kids from their one- or two-parent homes even when things are desperate there.

Finally, we believe that America is not paying attention to her kids. Children have the worst institutions (witness the number of federal court cases involving children's mental health facilities). Children's services and education budgets usually get whatever dollars are left over from building highways and waging wars. If we are indeed a child-oriented culture and nation, then the chasm between that ideology and our practices is becoming increasingly wider. Child abuse, infant mortality, and crimes against children are increasing. (Granted, so is the amount of money spent to report such unspeakable acts.) However, there is very little movement toward improving children's institutions in light of these statistics. Inadequate schools, children's hospitals, and playgrounds bear witness to our failure to practice our child-centered ideology.

Divorced fathers have important roles to play. They have to be vigilant to insure that their kids get a good start in life. Equally as important, there are going to be more divorced dads around. You have to become a model for others.

# Bestsellers from Berkley
## The books you've been hearing about—and want to read

\_\_ **CHILDREN OF POWER** 04478-5—$2.75
Susan Richards Shreve

\_\_ **DUKE OF DECEPTION** 04660-5—$2.75
Geoffrey Wolff

\_\_ **HIGH GLOSS** 04542-0—$2.50
Peter Engel

\_\_ **ABINGDON'S** 04479-3—$2.50
Michael French

\_\_ **THE THIRD WORLD WAR:**
**AUGUST 1985** 04477-7—$2.95
General Sir John Hackett, et al.

\_\_ **SELF-PORTRAIT** 04485-8—$2.75
Gene Tierney, with Mickey Herskowitz

\_\_ **THE WINNER'S CIRCLE** 04500-5—$2.50
Charles Paul Conn

\_\_ **MOMMIE DEAREST** 04444-0—$2.75
Christina Crawford

\_\_ **NURSE** 04685-0—$2.75
Peggy Anderson

\_\_ **THE SIXTH COMMANDMENT** 04271-5—$2.75
Lawrence Sanders

\_\_ **MANHATTAN** 04294-4—$2.50
Neal Travis

\_\_ **THE HEALERS** 04451-3—$2.75
Gerald Green